EVERYDAY GOURMET

# THE TRAVELING GOURMAND SERIES

1. ***The Gluten-Free Way***: *My Way*, by William Maltese & Adrienne Z. Milligan
2. ***Back of the Boat Gourmet Cooking***: *Afloat—Pool-Side—Backyard*, by Bonnie Clark & William Maltese
3. ***William Maltese's Wine Taster's Diary***: *Spokane/Pullman Washington Wine Region*, by William Maltese
4. ***In Search of the Perfect Pinot G!*** *Australia's Mornington Peninsula: William Maltese's Wine Taster's Guide #2*, by A. B. Gayle & William Maltese
5. ***Whole Wheat for Food Storage***: *Recipes for Unground Wheat*, by Michael R. Collings & Judith Collings
6. ***Even Gourmands Have to Diet***: *It's Just Food, People!*, by Bonnie Clark and William Maltese
7. ***Dinner with Cecile and William***: *A Cookbook*, by Cecile Charles and William Maltese
8. ***The Pot Thickens***: *Recipes from the Kitchens of Writers and Readers*, edited by Victor J. Banis
9. ***Get-Real Vegan Desserts***: *Vegan Recipes for the Rest of Us*, by Christina-Marie "Sexy Vegan Mama" Wright and William Maltese
10. ***Everyday Gourmet***: *A Memoir*, by William Maltese and Bonnie Clark

# EVERYDAY GOURMET

## A MEMOIR

WILLIAM MALTESE &

BONNIE CLARK

THE BORGO PRESS
MMXIII

EVERYDAY GOURMET

Copyright © 2013 by William Maltese and Bonnie Clark

FIRST EDITION

Published by Wildside Press LLC

www.wildsidebooks.com

# DEDICATION

To Bonnie Clark, without whom I would have been hard-pressed to bring to realization so many of the recipes in this book which, while well-remembered by me, weren't physically written down at the time.

And—

To Bruce Clark, whose input can sometimes be overlooked but never should be.

# CONTENTS

INTRODUCTION . . . . . . . . . . . . . . . . . .9
IN A STEW AS TO WHAT TO COOK? . . . . . 11
IRISH PUBS AND GRUB . . . . . . . . . . . . . 15
TORTILLA-SERAPE...YOUR BEAN BURGER . 19
WINING, DINING, AND BULLFIGHTING . . . 23
YES, IT'S CHICKEN, BUT... . . . . . . . . . . . 27
PADUA, PACIANO, (WATER) POLO, AND
    PASTA. . . . . . . . . . . . . . . . . . . . . . . 33
ADVANTAGING HUMPTY-DUMPTY. . . . . . 37
TOSSED BOSC . . . . . . . . . . . . . . . . . . . 41
PIGGING OUT ON PORKY. . . . . . . . . . . . 45
FAMILY JEWELS . . . . . . . . . . . . . . . . . . 49
IT'S OKAY TO HAM IT UP WITH HAM. . . . 53
PONDERING THE POTATO . . . . . . . . . . . 57
CATARACTS, COWBOYS, AND
    CHATEAUBRIAND . . . . . . . . . . . . . . . 61

"SIMPLICITY, THE UTTER SOPHISTICATION" . . . . . . . . . . . . . . . 65
SCOTCH SCOTCH IF YOU'RE SCOTCH . . . . 69
WHEN GIVEN A LEMON IN LIFE…MAKE LEMONADE, OR…. . . . . . . . . . . . . . . 73
SURF'S UP…FORMALITY ISN'T . . . . . . . . 77
BEYOND BOOKS…BERLIN, AND BEER . . . . 81
TOTO, I DON'T THINK WE'RE IN KANSAS ANYMORE. . . . . . . . . . . . . . . . . . . 85
GOBBLER, GOBBLE…BANG! GOBBLE. . . . . 89
GOOD GRUB WITHOUT GALLIVANTING . . 93
BEER, BEER…HERE, HERE!. . . . . . . . . . . 97
TIME FOR BEANY!. . . . . . . . . . . . . . . . 101
SAUCY APPLE-OF-MY-EYE . . . . . . . . . . 107
NO NEED TO "CHUCK" IT. . . . . . . . . . . 111
ADVANTAGING BOG AND PATCH. . . . . . 117
WHERE? AND EATING WHAT? . . . . . . . 121
CIAO, COLUMBUS!. . . . . . . . . . . . . . . 125
EATING THE VOLCANO. . . . . . . . . . . . 129
PICNICKING AT CHÂTEAU DE VERSAILLES. . . . . . . . . . . . . . . . 133
ABOUT THE AUTHORS . . . . . . . . . . . . 139

# INTRODUCTION

As many who have traveled a good deal, and eaten a good deal, and drunk a good deal, I have a tendency to remember, and remember well, a good deal of those times in my life when I've experienced truly memorable dining experiences.

On such occasions, if the opportunity presented itself, I've been known to persuade the host, hostess, or their representatives in their respective kitchens, to part with the recipes for those items on their menus that I've particularly enjoyed, whether such culinary blueprints were merely jotted down on the spot, on wine-splotched coasters, or neatly printed out for me by computer and then mailed to me at some later date.

On many an occasion, however, for whatever the reason (secret family recipe, an improvising chef, too drunk to think straight, etcetera), I've found myself having left the scene of an event, savoring the experience of it, but without benefit of any physical recipe in-hand with which to recreate the memory at some later date. Therefore, I've found myself, often all on my own, working from memory, when attempting to replicate, in my own kitchen, some much-enjoyed item initially eaten elsewhere.

Not by way of bragging about my cooking expertise, taste buds, and keen sense of smell, but I have, more often than not, come pretty close to duplicating a good many of those dishes that I've set out to duplicate. Not by way of complaining about my lack of cooking expertise, taste buds, and keen sense of smell, but I have, on more occasions than I care to admit, ended up not quite satisfied.

When writing this book, I have, as in the past, called upon the expertise of my fellow gourmet, gourmand, and co-author, Bonnie Clark, and her husband Bruce, for whatever the necessary tweaking necessary to end up, as nearly as possible, with what I remember eating in the first place. Without their assistance and the skill-set of their cooking expertise, taste buds, and keen senses of smell, there's no doubt in my mind that this book would have turned out far less satisfactory to me than it has. And for that, I extend to them my deepest heart-felt appreciation.

# IN A STEW AS TO WHAT TO COOK?

Just because three of my cookbooks, published by Wildside/Borgo Press, now include "gourmet" or "gourmand" in their titles (*BACK OF THE BOAT GOURMET COOKING, EVEN GOURMANDS HAVE TO DIET*, and *EVERYDAY GOURMET: A MEMOIR*, all written with Bonnie Clark), don't be confused into thinking that I'm someone who continually indulges in only high-end dining. In point of fact, my definition of gourmet has always been, and remains, merely "good" food; a gourmand merely someone who enjoys the eating.

While I do prepare the likes of Beef Wellington, and filet steak, coated with pâté de foie gras and duxelles, all nicely wrapped up for presentation in puff pastry and baked, now I'm merely going to deal with a French peasant stew, despite it's often intimidating name—boeuf bourguignon. I do so, because I've had the misfortune of spending my winter in the Pacific Northwest corner of the United States, where chilly weather has seen me, more often than not, seek consolation in a full-bodied and robust meal that can make me feel all warm inside and momentarily able to forget the bleak weather just outside the door.

The dish originated in the Burgundy (Bourgogne) region of what is today eastern France, and is prepared with beef braised in a red wine (traditionally red Burgundy); broth, more often than not, flavored with garlic. Often, pearl onions and mushrooms are added toward the end of the cooking.

Originally, the meat was provided with lardons (strips of fat) but modern beef is usually tender enough, and with enough natural marbling, to exclude this time consuming step; these days, cubed bacon produces the initial cooking fat and for adding at the end.

### Beef Bourguignon (aka French Stew)

Preheat oven to 325°F

8 oz bacon, cut into ½-inch pieces
3 lb stew meat (or beef roast), cut into 1½-inch chunks
1 tsp salt
½ tsp fresh ground pepper
¼ c flour
2 garlic cloves, minced
3 c Burgundy wine
1 c beef stock
1 sprig of fresh thyme (or ½ tsp dried leaves)
4 large carrots cut into 1-inch slices
1 lb mushrooms, cut in half
2 TBS butter (or olive oil)
½ lb pearl onions, fresh peeled or frozen

To thicken, if needed:

2 TBS butter, softened
2 TBS flour

In a 6-quart Dutch oven, sauté the bacon over medium low heat, until brown and crisp. Set bacon aside. Discard all but 3 TBS of fat from pan.

Heat pan over medium high heat. Sprinkle stew meat with salt and pepper and some of the ¼ c flour. Toss lightly. Brown stew meat in the bacon fat in small batches until brown on all sides—do not over crowd. Remove browned stew meat and set aside.

To the vacated pan, add minced garlic and ALL that remains of the ¼ c flour. Cook for 30 seconds.

Turn pan to high heat. Deglaze the pan with the Burgundy wine for about 1 minute, scraping the bottom of the pan. Add the stew meat, bacon, stock, and thyme.

Cover and bake in oven for 2½ hours.

Add carrots.

Sauté the mushrooms in about 2 TBS butter (or olive oil), for about 7 minutes, until golden brown. Add mushrooms and pearl onions to pot.

If sauce needs thickening, use above "thickening"

ingredients by—

Mashing with a fork the 2 TBS flour with the 2 TBS butter; removing Dutch oven from the oven; and whisking, a ½ tsp of the flour-butter mixture at a time, into the sauce, until blended.

Cover and continue cooking (about another 1 hour) until meat is fork-tender.

Makes about 10 servings.

NOTE: As the author of the *WILLIAM MALTESE'S WINE TASTER'S DIARY* series of books, I usually recommend accompanying this hearty meal with a nice red wine...in this case a 2002 BV Cabernet Sauvignon.

# IRISH PUBS AND GRUB

Over the years, I've noted a definite divide in my eating and drinking preferences that, more often than not, require someone to observe me both in the U.S. and when abroad in order for them to detect the difference.

In the U.S., you're most likely to find me hanging out in wine-tasting rooms (private or public), and/or cocktail lounges, rather than bellying up to the bar with "the boys" in some local tavern. When you're invited to dinner at my U.S. home, you'll usually find me serving up more than one kind of wine, but you'll have to look far and wide for a bottle of beer. There's just something about the majority of North American beers (and I'm not just talking the watered-down Lites), that, in my opinion (possibly because of my having been raised on the heartier brews of Europe), find me very seldom searching any of them out. Granted, North American stores now provide a whole assortment of imported beers that would likely satisfy even my discerning palate, but somehow picking up a six-pack of Bavarian Weihenstephaner Hefeweissbler at my local U.S. grocery store just doesn't do "it" for me enough to see beer provide much of an impact on my wining and dining experiences when hunkered down in the States.

However, set me down in any of the great brewing locales of the world...say, in Germany, during Ocktober Fest...and/or in Ireland...at just about any time of the year...and it's quite another story. Suddenly, I'm thrust into pub-crawler mode that will see me off (always with a designated driver, of course), to check out just about every biergarten or pub within easy (and sometimes not-so-easy) access.

Over the years, I've concluded that it's not just the more intense beers of Europe that so attract me, but, also, the food, by way of snacks, that often can be had in accompaniment, usually far more diverse and interesting than the usual fare of pickled hard-boiled eggs or micro-waved "whatever" that are their U.S. equivalents. By way of example, here's the recipe of a particularly well-remembered Irish-pub snack that, since my first sampling on-site in Ireland, has, with only slight variations from the original, provided my friends and me with some very choice moments of enjoyable eating.

### Open-Face Irish Pub Sandwich

8 sweet or hot sausages—not smoked
2 bottles of Guinness Beer—enough to cover sausages
2 red bell peppers, cored, and seeded, cut into ¼-inch rings
2 yellow bell peppers, cored and seeded, cut into

¼-inch rings
2 TBS olive oil
1 medium onion, cut into ¼-inch rings (prevent onion slices from separating by securing them horizontally with a wooden toothpicks).
2 TBS Worcestershire sauce
2 tsps balsamic vinegar
4 elongated ("hoagie") rolls
1 tomato, sliced

Simmer sausages in the Guinness Beer over medium-low heat for about 10 minutes. Drain on paper towels.

In a bowl, toss the red and yellow bell-pepper rings with 1½ TBS oil.

Brush onion rings with the remaining ½ TBS olive oil.

Over medium high heat, grill sausages until nicely brown and cooked through.

Grill veggies on well-oiled grill, or in batches in a well-seasoned or oiled grill pan, over medium-high heat, for about 3 minutes, each side. Transfer to a bowl and toss lightly in Worcestershire Sauce and balsamic vinegar. Discard toothpicks from onions.

Halve grill sausages, lengthwise.

Halve buns, lengthwise, and grill, cut sides down, for about 1 minute—don't overcook or you'll risk dryness.

Evenly divide sausages, bell peppers, and onions on each halved roll.

Garnish each open-faced sandwich with fresh tomato slices.

Makes four sizable servings!

NOTE: Nothing beats drinking a bottle of Guinness with this, especially when in Ireland. Stateside, I often serve a Washington State Vintner's Reserve, World Vineyard Collection, Sangiovese.

# TORTILLA-SERAPE...
# YOUR BEAN BURGER

For a number of reasons, I've spent a good deal of time in Mexico over the years.

Firstly, I'm a lover of warmth and sunshine. I was born and raised in the Pacific Northwest region of the United States which, to this very day, is well-known for being a tad skimpy by way of toasty summers. Mexican resorts, like Acapulco, Puerto Vallarta, and Cabo San Lucas—ask any college kids on Spring break—can usually be counted upon to provide tanning rays at just about any time of the year.

Secondly, Mexico is convenient, being just south of the U.S. border.

Thirdly, Mexico not only offers up the kind of adventures had in visiting foreign locales, missing in places like the Florida Keys or Hawaii, but offers my two years of paid-for Spanish-language classes the opportunity to come to my aid by way of communication with the locals.

Fourthly, as an aficionado of bullfights, I've discovered Mexico is the closest country in which to find a corrida without having to head due east, across the wide Atlantic, to reach the shores of Portugal.

Fifthly, I have this thing for ruins, and Mexico abounds in enough of them to keep me trekking through different ones on each and every visit.

Sixthly, but far from last, there's always the gastronomical delights of Mexican cuisine, not only had from its finer dining establishments but from its plethora of street stalls, found just about anywhere, and everywhere, like the next recipe which I ran across as served up by a street vendor in Cancún, a city in which, at the time, I was catching some rays before heading off to hike more of the Yucatán Peninsula.

Although, yes, I have provided a few embellishments of my own, including the title's play on words, "Tortilla-Seraped", based upon the fact that the tortilla gets "wrapped" around the sandwich contents like a serape often gets wrapped around a Mexican. And, yes, while I DO know that "Greek" Yogurt is hardly indicative of Mexico, I have, through much experimentation, discovered, as have my guests, that substituting Greek Yogurt for the ordinary yogurt I initially used when preparing this dish does provide an additional certain "something".

## Tortilla-Seraped Black Chipolte Bean Burritos

4 Chipotle Black Bean patties (such as "Morning Star Farms")
4 large non-fat, low-carb, high-fiber, whole-wheat tortillas
4 TBS jalapeño Greek Yogurt
8 TBS fresh pico de gallo
4 TBS grated cheddar cheese (optional)

Cook Chipotle Black Bean patties according to directions on package.

Heat tortillas.

Spread yogurt on tortillas.

Cut the patties in half and arrange two patty halves onto one side of each tortilla.

Top each piece of patty with pico de gallo and grated cheese.

Wrap un-piled half of the tortillas over filled parts to form sandwiches.

Cut each sandwich into 3 pieces.

Serve immediately.

NOTE: I've been known to serve this with cold Mexican beer (it's almost always Negra Modelo—

although Corona is a good choice). By way of white wine, I usually opt for chilled Idaho State Ste Chapelle "Soft White" (a favorite of mine).

# WINING, DINING, AND BULLFIGHTING

If you're a fan of bullfighting (which I am)...and if you've the time and money to spare (as I once did) to go to Mexico and follow the bullfights for a whole season, between November and April, selecting from among the fights occurring every Sunday afternoon in over 220 of that country's bullrings (which it was once my good fortune to do)...then, by chance, you may eventually meet enough fellow aficionados (as I did) to get invited to one or more of the country's bull-breeding ranches.

The Mexican state of Tlaxcala has been the center of Mexican bullfighting ever since Cortes and his fellow conquistadors stopped off there on their way to conquer the Aztec in Tenochtitlan, and is home to over forty "ganaderias", including the country's most famous ranch, Ganaderia La Laguna de Terrenate, established (with cows from Tepeyahualco and a breeding bull from Ibarra) in 1908; the ranch has produced more bulls for the Plaza de Toros in Mexico City than any other supplier.

It's a fascinating experience for those who have only

been to U.S. ranches to learn how all of the bulls on Mexican gandarias are never approached on foot lest they become too accustomed to seeing people that way—before a matador does just that in the bullring.

Interesting, too, is watching the tientas in the corridas of the gandarias where full-grown bulls aren't usually "put to the cape", rather heifers, since it's the ongoing belief of most breeders that the bravery of the mothers determine the bravery of their offspring.

Usually following a tienta, there's a meal to be enjoyed, and it was during one of these that I first became acquainted with the dish that follows.

### Corrida Frittata

7 eggs
2 TSP milk (for the diet-conscious, skim works for me)
½ tsp salt
¼ tsp fresh ground pepper
2 TSP olive oil
1 lb asparagus, trimmed and cut into ½-inch pieces
½ Roma tomato, sliced
Pinch of salt
3 oz Fontina Cheese, diced

Preheat broiler.

Whisk eggs, milk, salt, and pepper together in bowl. Set aside.

Heat oil in a 10-inch oven-proof skillet, preferable

nonstick, over medium heat. Sauté the asparagus until crisp-tender, about 2 minutes. Turn heat to medium-high.

Add diced tomatoes and a pinch of salt and sauté for 2 more minutes.

Add egg mixture and cook until eggs start to set. Reduce heat to medium-low.

Sprinkle cheese on top and cook for about 2 more minutes, until frittata is almost set (top will still be a bit runny).

Put skillet under broiler and broil until top is set and golden brown, about 5 minutes.

Remove from broiler and let stand for 2 minutes.

Garnish with the tomato slices.

Serves 6.

This is nicely accompanied by a salad of strawberries, bleu-cheese crumbles, and candied walnuts, on a bed of romaine lettuce, tossed in huckleberry vinaigrette... with crisp garlic toast strips on the side.

NOTE: Egg dishes, such as this one, usually have me serving crisp, dry white wines in accompaniment (from Mexico or otherwise), and I've successfully paired this with Rieslings, even Chardonnays, as well as, most preferably, various Champagnes and/or Sparkling Wines. Then, again, there are some people, and that may well be you and any number of your guests, who simply don't think *any* wine goes well with asparagus.

# YES, IT'S CHICKEN, BUT...

I was at the train station, waiting to embark for the three-hour ride to the ancient once-lost-now-found Incan mountain retreat of Machu Picchu, Peru. It was pre-dawn, only because the sun hadn't yet made its official appearance by actually topping the snowy high-Andean peaks in the East, only just beginning to paintbrush that horizon with a faint shade of blushing pink.

That my point of departure was Cuzco, a city with more than a quarter-million people, made the accompanying sounds of unseen crowing roosters, all in herald of the upcoming dawn, genuinely incongruous, especially to this city boy who wasn't used to any barnyard sounds occurring—morning, noon, or night—in U.S. cities of far less population.

Once on board the train that began its series of switch-backs that would take us up one side of the mountainous bowl enclosing Cuzco, even to a higher elevation than the city's 11,000+ feet, then slide us down the other side to the still-lofty Incan Citadel, at 8,000 feet, I could look out the window and get up-close views of many Peruvian shanties with backyards whose hard-packed dirt provided occasional views of chickens...which made my traveling companion genuinely ecstatic.

"God, do you know how long it's been since I've seen a free-range chicken?" she said, more than once. "I've not seen one since I was a kid back on the farm. And, let me tell you, there is no comparison to eating one when it's in a contest with one of those hormone-laden mutations we get in our local U.S. grocery stores."

In fact, she had me so convinced of what I'd been missing, that when I, later, noticed there was chicken on the menu of our hotel in Machu Picchu, I made specific inquiry of the chef, who assured me the chicken in question was, indeed, free-range; we ordered it. Only to find ourselves served up with probably the toughest bird I'd ever eaten, or, for that matter, have eaten since. All of that free-ranging in a country where every morsel of food had to be fought over, even in competition with the local human population, had left our poor bird nothing more than muscle, sinew, gristle, and bones.

Of course, since then, having been able to access free-ranging chickens that have actually existed within environments where food for them is plentiful, I've come to realize that my companion on that train to Machu Picchu hadn't been wrong when saying that they DO taste differently (aka better) than their store-bought counterparts, especially to food purists.

In fact, it was just one such free-range chicken, literally chased down on a privately owned South Pacific atoll, killed, gutted, and plucked for an evening roast on a beach bonfire that provided my first sampling of Beer-Butt chicken, the recipe for which follows. Not that a free-range chicken is required. Frankly, I've had consistently great results, since, with the mass-produced plump fryers I've picked up at local U.S. grocery stores.

### Beer-Butt Chicken

Prepare rub:

1 TBS Paprika
1 TBS Garlic salt
1 TBS Onion powder
1 TBS Salt
1 TBS Pepper
Cayenne Pepper, to taste (optional)

Set rub aside.

1 can of beer (12 oz)
1 chicken (approximately 4 lb)
Olive oil
2 c of wood chips (preferably hickory, or cherry), soaked for 1 hour in water (or beer), then drained.

Pop the beer-can tab. Dump ½ of the beer over the wood chips. Use a church-key opener to make 2 additional holes in the top of the can. Set can and its remaining beer aside.

Remove giblets from chicken body cavity and save them for some other time. Remove and discard whatever excess skin and fat you find inside the chicken cavities. Rinse the chicken, inside and out, under cold running water. Drain. Blot dry, inside and out.

Sprinkle some of the rub inside the chicken body and neck cavities.

Drizzle the olive oil over the outside of the bird to coat the skin.

Sprinkle rub over the outside of the chicken. (If you have remaining rub, funnel it through one of the holes in the beer-can lid, not being concerned by any resulting foam).

Hold the chicken upright, and sit its body's cavity firmly down and over the beer can, pulling the chicken's legs forward to provide, along with the can, a tripod that allows the bird to remain erect.

Tuck the tips of the chicken wings.

If using a gas grill, place wood chips in smoker box or smoker pouch, preheat grill to high until chips begin to smoke, then turn down to medium. Put a drip pan under chicken.

Place erect chicken (affixed on beer can) to center of grate (over drip pan) away from the main heat. Cover and cook until the skin is dark golden and crisp (1 to 1½ hours). If using charcoal, you'll need to add more charcoal after about an hour of cooking.

If chicken skin starts too brown too quickly, turn heat down or move chicken farther away from the coals.

Using tongs, grip the visible part of the beer can, and the chicken, to transfer the chicken in an upright position onto a platter. Let it remain there for about five minutes, and, then, very carefully, being sure not to spill any hot beer still in the can (or burn yourself), remove the bird from the beer can. Cut chicken into halves or quarters.

Serves 2 – 4

Should you want to do this over an open fire, merely start your grated camp fire, let it (and charcoal, if you so desire) burn down to glowing coals. Place upright chicken-on-its-beer-can on the grate, cover bird with aluminum foil. Cook.

NOTE: I have a tendency just to serve beer with this dish, although if I choose to make it more formal, I invariably opt for a Pinot Noir. The dish, being wood-smoked, lends itself to experimentations with reds; Pinot Noirs having proved, in my opinion, to be the best.

## PADUA, PACIANO, (WATER) POLO, AND PASTA

I was in Italy, again, this time busy writing my mainstream romantic/adventure novel, *VANESSA IN WHITE MARBLE*. I was checked in to a small, family-owned hotel in Padua, spending all of my time, when not researching or writing my book, taking in the local museums and ruins, or just sitting in local cafés, drinking Cappuccino or wine (depending upon the time of day). Also, of course, I was constantly kept busy eating fine food, including non-stop snacking on enormous bowls of gelato, and watching some of the most beautiful people in the world pass by. Water polo was the farthest thought from my mind, until I was introduced to Paciano one afternoon in the lobby of my hotel. Grandson of the hotel proprietors, Paciano was not only one of the most attractive young men I've ever seen (Italian or otherwise), but, as it turned out, was goalie of a local water-polo team.

I wasn't long listening to Paciano enthusiastically expound upon his sport and how top players from around the world actually came specifically to Italy to play because of the top-notch competition afforded and the money offered, before I became a whole lot more interested in Italian-played water polo than I'd ever been before. When I was offered comp tickets to a game that was being played that very evening, I jumped at the chance, needing very little persuasion to see in real life, wearing only Speedos, the same fine anatomical specimens of Italian manhood, which, up until then, I'd been so admiring in the statuary of Italian museums, or in the latest fashions always to be seen on Italian sidewalks. The resulting experience was so enjoyable that I've since made it a point, if anywhere in Italy during the water-polo season (March thru May), to try and work in a game or two. During that time frame, not only is the Italian League in the middle of its competition, but the European C of Champions is, also, going on, featuring the club champions of all the European water-polo teams who play at home and away-games in the countries of the competition, including Italy.

Additional fond memories of my first Italian water-polo match was the win by Paciano's team, my joining its members for the celebratory festivities afterwards, and the early-morning insistence, by my favorite water-polo goalie, that I join him for a late-night snack in my hotel's deserted kitchen. While he humbly insisted that he was nowhere near the cook his grandmother was, he did admit to her having taught him a few culinary tricks, one of which was what to do with the left-over ravioli he soon had removed from the refrigerator.

While, afterwards, I thought, perhaps, that meal was made to seem so delicious by the circumstances, I've since tried the recipe enough times to know that, despite the simplicity of the dish, it's pretty much just as enjoyable every time I make it, even when, left-over fresh ravioli is seldom as available in my refrigerator as I would wish; my having discovered that frozen packages of ravioli, especially the ones I've recently found at Costco, provide a suitably delicious compromise.

### Goalie Ravioli

16 cheese-and-spinach ravioli (fresh or frozen)
2 TBS olive oil
2 to 3 garlic cloves, minced
3 oz goat cheese
Parmesan cheese, freshly grated
2 TBS fresh parsley, minced

Cook ravioli according to directions on the package.

While ravioli is cooking, heat olive oil over low heat and simmer minced garlic until a light golden brown, stirring often, and being careful it doesn't burn.

Just before the ravioli is done...whisk goat cheese into garlic-and-oil with enough water (¼ – ½ c) from the ravioli to make a sauce.

Drain ravioli; add to prepared sauce; mix.

Sprinkle with the Parmesan cheese and parsley.

Serve immediately.

Makes 4 to 5 servings.

NOTE: I remember the days wherein I figured a white wine would be the best match for any vegetable-and-cheese based ravioli, and that theory has since proved true, as regards some of the more buttery Chardonnays and/or full-bodied Pinot Gris. However, do try to avoid less robust whites or risk disappointment. More often than not, these days, I rely upon the richness of the dish to allow me companioning it with any light-to-medium red wine...although nothing too in-your-face or you overwhelm what you're eating.

# ADVANTAGING HUMPTY-DUMPTY

*Humpty Dumpty sat on a wall,
Humpty Dumpty had a great fall.
All the king's horses and all the king's men
Couldn't put Humpty together again.*
                —Old English nursery rhyme

I was "doing" Italy and Greece, having joined a group that included two fellow Americans, Harry and Charlotte, both from San Francisco. It was nearing the completion of our tour, our having drinks on the rooftop of our Athens hotel, the Parthenon-topped Acropolis looking fantastic in the distance, despite it's shroud of smog, when Harry asked the inevitable question: "Where, William, do you think you might end up next in the world?"

I'd pretty much decided upon England, the result of a novel I thought it might be fun to write (since published as *A CONSPIRACY OF RAVENS*), if the rumor proved true that there really was a flock of ravens housed within the grounds of The Tower of London, the birds wings regularly clipped to keep them from exiting the premises lest an old legend come true that prophesied their departure would herald the downfall of the British Empire.

As luck would have it, likewise proving what a small world it really is, Harry had first heard the legend directly from an old friend of his, a retired Yeoman Warder who had been one of the very Beefeaters (an erroneous nickname probably having originally resulted from meat once part of the daily rations for the men on duty at the Tower) "of Her Majesty's Royal Palace and Fortress the Tower of London and Member of the Sovereign's Body Guard of the Yeoman Guard Extraordinary." Harry said he'd be happy to contact his friend, next time I was in London, to see if there was anyone presently on duty who could provide me with a personalized tour.

That was why, less than a year later, Harry, Charlotte, and I, were not only being shown around The Tower and its environs but were within pecking distance of the seven clipped-winged ravens in residence at the time. There had been eight up until three days before when one of the birds had been banished, as had others in the past, for "conduct unbecoming a Tower Resident."

The next day, we were in a hired car, headed for Henley on Thames (site of the yearly Regatta) to give thanks to Harry's friend who had made the arrangements for us to visit The Tower the previous day. It was while we were all sitting on the rough-stone patio of the retired Yeoman Warder's retirement "cottage" (whose doorways were all so low that they required our constant ducking or some nasty head-whacking), that I was first served the following baked-eggs dish of which I've since become particularly fond.

### Queen's-Man Baked Eggs

(Having previously mentioned free-range chickens, let me say that eggs from the same are more flavorful than ordinary eggs).

1 tsp garlic, finely minced
1 tsp fresh thyme leaves, finely minced
1 tsp chives, finely minced
2 TBS fresh parsley, minced
3 TBS Parmesan cheese, freshly grated
4 TBS milk, (skim, or whole, or 2%, or cream)
2 tsps butter, unsalted
12 extra-large eggs, (free-range when available)
Salt, preferably Napastyle® Gray Salt
Black pepper, freshly ground

Place the rack about 6 inches from the broiler. Preheat the broiler for 5 minutes.

Combine the garlic, thyme, chives, parsley, and cheese. Set aside.

Put 4 individual gratin dishes on a baking sheet; place 1 TBS of milk (or cream), and ½ tsp of butter in each dish. Place under the broiler for about 3 minutes, or until bubbly.

As milk and butter are heating, crack 3 eggs into each of 4 cups or small bowls, being careful not to break yolks. Have these ready to go when milk and butter are hot.

Quickly, but carefully, pour 3 eggs into each of the 4 individual gratin dishes.

Divide herb and cheese mixture into four equal parts and sprinkle over eggs. Salt and pepper to taste.

Place dishes back under broiler, cooking until eggs are almost done, about 5 to 6 minutes. The eggs will continue to cook after they are out of the oven, so DON'T overcook.

Serve with toasted French bread.

NOTE: This is something I always used to serve with a drink made of ½ Champagne and ½ orange juice (which is what the retired Yeoman and his wife served with it). Whenever serving it, though, with pear salad as a side dish (see the very next recipe), I, now, usually accompany it with "Pear Bellinis"—equal parts pear nectar, pear brandy, and chilled dry champagne over crushed ice.

# TOSSED BOSC

It hasn't always been necessary for me to find recipes in Italy, while eating late-night snacks with an Italian water-polo goalie...in Mexico, at the buffet table of a famous matador's hacienda, after a corrida...in Ireland, pub-crawling with friends...or having baked eggs prepared by a retired Tower of London "beefeater" and his wife in Henley on Thames. Many of my favorite dishes of all time, as a matter of fact, remain those that my dear mum whipped up in her lifetime, and those of my grandmother before her, many of those appearing in my three cookbooks—*THE GLUTEN FREE-WAY: MY WAY* (with Adrienne Z. Milligan)...*BACK OF THE BOAT GOURMET COOKING*, and *EVEN GOURMANDS HAVE TO DIET* (both with Bonnie Clark)...as well as my already contracted *THE GOURMET HUCKLEBERRY*, due out later this year.

Other fertile sources, of course, have always been friends and relatives with whom I've been able to eat (drink), and enjoy many an enjoyable evening, starting when I was very young.

Long-time friends of my parents owned a working farm in the Wenatchee region of central Washington

State, U.S.A., where we used to visit several times a year. The farm was a genuinely exotic and fascinating place to a city-born-and-bred boy, like me; although, I've since learned that many a farm boy...not nearly as appreciative as I of milk and cream directly from a cow; fresh vegetables directly from the garden; duck killed, plucked, and roasted the very same day; eggs still warm from the hen that laid them...are just as excited about getting to the exoticism of the big city to eat at the fast-food places found there.

Every trip to Jesse and Louise's farm, whenever the area's fruit crop was ripe, saw at least one afternoon wherein a picnic basket was packed, and all of us headed off on the half-an-hour trek through the orchard with its fresh fruit, usually apples as big and glossy-red as ever tempted Snow White, drooped invitingly from leafy-green branches. Wenatchee, in those days, was even more famous for its apples than it is for its wines today.

Our final destination was one lone pear tree that was assigned a space twice as roomy as any apple tree in the same orchard. The pear tree was big, it was gnarly, and, frankly, it looked so old that the first time I saw it, I figured it and its brownish fruit (complete with russeting), were simultaneously on their last legs, especially since I was informed that Jesse's grandfather had brought the original sapling from the old world in the 1830s. However, that was merely my introduction to Bosc Pears, naturally brown, wherein before I'd only been familiar with pleasantly yellow Bartletts.

Ever after that first picnic—Jesse having plucked several ripe Bosc pears directly from the tree to toss them to Louise...who washed them with water from the canteen and dried them...fresh salad greens, then, dumped from a plastic bag onto each of our plates... topped with freshly sliced Bosc pears, along with a few additional garnishes—I've been won over by this genuinely pleasant but simple dish.

I still get nostalgic, thinking of my parents and me, on Jesse and Louise's farm, out in that sun-dappled Wenatchee orchard, dining on salad made with fresh Bosc pears plucked directly from the tree.

**Pear-Orchard Salad**

Huckleberry Vinaigrette (You can home-make this from the "Berry Vinaigrette" recipe in *EVEN GOURMANDS HAVE TO DIET*)
4 c romaine leaves, torn into bite-size pieces
2 fresh Bosc (or Bartlett) pears
1 oz bleu cheese, crumbled
4 tsps walnuts, toasted and chopped
4 TBS cranberries, dried

Put ½ c of Huckleberry Vinaigrette in the bottom of a large bowl.

Add the romaine leaves and toss.

Divide into 4 plates.

Core but do not peel the pears.

Slice pears lengthways and divide slices among the 4 plates.

Sprinkle ¼ oz blue cheese, crumbled, on each serving.

Sprinkle 1 tsp walnuts, toasted and chopped, on each serving.

Sprinkle 1 TBS of cranberries, dried, on each serving.

Serves 4.

NOTE: Many of my guests expect a white wine with this, but I usually surprise them by serving a Cabernet Sauvignon. Admittedly, though, if I'm just serving the salad, pretty much by itself, as a light lunch, I'm fond of pairing it with Xante Pear Liqueur which is very expensive, although cheaper brands will still please a less discerning palate. And, of course, there's always "Champagne-with-Pear-Liqueur" (one tsp of Pear Liqueur, and one slice of peeled and cored ripe pear in a Champagne glass that's topped off with California Sparkling Wine), which is a drink I first tasted while visiting Chef Michael Chiarello's vineyard in Napa Valley, California, U.S.A.

# PIGGING OUT ON PORKY

Long before that probably well-remembered ad campaign that heralded "the *other* white meat", I've been a particular fan of pork, my father having introduced me to it by grilling genuinely thick chops that to this day have me sticking my nose up at those seemingly paper-thin cuts sold in supermarkets as "breakfast meat".

I've gone out of my way to sample pork, the world around, even having hunted wild boar in South Korea. There's really nothing more caveman-satisfactory than chowing down on something personally killed for the larder (although the sinewy boar in question was decidedly less than tender).

I've dined on loin of wild boar, caramelized vegetable and marjoram jus gras with mini suet pudding, at The Gallivant Hotel, Camber, East Sussex, England.

In Hawaii, I watched a large pit dug in the ground, and then lined with banana leaves. Saw lava rocks heated over open flames until exceedingly hot and then placed in the pit. Observed a whole cleaned pig, seasoned with Hawaiian sea salt, get placed in the hole, covered with more greenery, and finally heaped with soil for eight hours of cooking to emerge tender and succulent. Then, I headed off to Bora Bora where I experienced the South Sea suckling-pig equivalent at a traditional 'tamaaraa'.

When partying, back in my Seattle, Washington, "artsy-fartsy" days, the really "in" thing was to have your event catered by Trader Vic's that could be counted upon to serve up its marvelous version of crisp, savory, roasted piglet.

That said, I confess to having run across one exceedingly tasty pork dish while not even looking, rather while focused on the wines of California's Napa Valley region. Color me genuinely bowled over by the marvelous pork shoulder served by Chef Michael Chiarello during one of his dinners in his Chiarello Family Vineyards. As a result of which, I set out to try and duplicate what I'd tasted, succeeding in conjuring what has become an especially favorite pork recipe of mine.

### Cocoa Spice Pork Shoulder

*for Spice Rub:*

¼ c fennel seeds
1 TBS coriander seeds
1 TBS peppercorns
1 tsp red pepper flakes
3 TBS NapaStyle® sea salt
1 TBS ground cinnamon
3 TBS unsweetened cocoa powder

Over medium heat, in a small heavy skillet, toast fennel seeds, coriander seeds, and peppercorns.

Toss or stir frequently and watch closely so as not to burn.

Carefully, add pepper flakes, taking care not to inhale!

Toss or stir quickly so not to burn, 30 seconds or so, until they release their aroma.

Cool on a plate.

Grind (in a spice mill or coffee grinder).

Add to sea salt, ground cinnamon, and cocoa powder.

*for Roast Pork Shoulder:*

6 lb, whole, boneless, pork shoulder (butt)
4 TBS Spice Rub (See recipe above)

Preheat oven 275°F.

Open roast like a book and sprinkle about a TBS of Spice Rub on the inside.

Close roast and tie with kitchen twine.

Rub on remaining Spice Rub.

Place roast on a rack in a shallow roasting pan.

Cook until fork-tender (6½ - 7½ hours).

Let rest 15 minutes.

Remove tie.

Transfer roast to platter.

Don't carve; use a fork to pull meat into large chunks.

NOTE: By way of honoring what inspired me to come up with this pork dish, I always try to serve it with one of the truly very fine wines from the Napa Valley's exceptional Chiarello Family Vineyard. While Michael served his pork dish with the family's Roux Old Vine Petit Sarah, I've always found the Chiarello Family Vineyard's Felicia Old Vine Zinfindel, with its hint of chocolate, more suited to the above-dish's cocoa-based rub. For those of you, however, with tighter budgets, try a Napa Valley Old Vine Zinfandel from Ravenswood Winery.

# FAMILY JEWELS

Sometimes, little gems, by way of recipes, can exist at my very kitchen doorway, for ages and ages, my taking seemingly forever to realize they're even there. Take for instance today's recipe for a salad I truly believed I was seeing and tasting for the very first time at a dinner hosted by my cousin and her husband.

These days, salads are something to which I pay particular attention, since I'm constantly involved in tasting and experimenting with all sorts of calorie-ridden foods for inclusion in my ongoing series of cookbooks. Most recently, I've been sampling vegan desserts for the book I'm writing with Christina-Marie "Sexy GonzoMama" Wright—vegan dessert, as it turns out, anything but non-fattening. As I have to be especially careful that I'm not pigging out all of the time, salads make ideal dining between bouts of sheer gluttony.

So, I commented as to how tasty and unusual the salad was. My cousin's response was an open-mouthed expression of disbelief, as she, then, proceeded to remind me it was the very same salad our dearly departed Aunt Dorthy had brought to most all of the family potluck get-togethers held in her lifetime. However, despite that heads-up, I still couldn't, and still can't, recall ever having seen, let alone ever having eaten that particular salad before then.

In my defense, those large family get-togethers to which I refer, including birthdays, have never been much my "thing". In that regard, I take after my parents, both non-drinkers, who would show up with us kids at such parties only to leave early, before any booze came out, or, if out, began to have its effect on those who were drinking it. Nonetheless, we usually stayed long enough to eat, so how Aunt Dorthy's salad escaped my attention remains something of a mystery. Possibly, I was just too young, in those days, to be all that interested in salads, if interested in them at all.

By the time I was off to university, then my three-years of service in the U.S. Army, and then off to see the rest of the world, I'd pretty much jettisoned family reunions and birthdays even when home visiting. By the time my grandparents had died, many other members of my extended family had gone their own ways, get-togethers not nearly as frequent as they once were. Anyway, that's my excuse, and I'm sticking to it.

As for discovering (or rediscovering) the salad in question—better late than never.

## Aunt Dorthy's Salad

Layer in a large bowl:

1 large head of iceberg lettuce, torn into bite-size pieces
5 or 6 large stalks of crisp celery, diced
1 small bunch scallions, thinly sliced, using tender part of the green
1 small can water chestnuts, sliced
1 (16-oz) package frozen petit peas, do not thaw

Cover with:

2 c good mayonnaise

Sprinkle with:

2 TSP sugar.

Without tossing, cover bowl tightly with plastic wrap and refrigerate overnight.

Just before serving, toss salad.

Then, without any additional tossing, layer on:

1 lb bacon, cooked crisp, chopped into small pieces
4-6 hard-boiled eggs, sliced (reserve one egg for garnish)
2 c cheddar cheese, grated

Garnish with sliced egg.

Still without additional tossing, serve immediately.

Serves 10-12.

NOTE: I know a lot of people who simply skip wine with any salad, finding any match-up way too difficult to manage. In the end, even I've discovered that any successful pairing of wine with salad, this salad included, usually boils down to individual taste. Usually, though, if just because of this salad's mayonnaise, I serve it with chilled Riesling. For some people, it, also, works with white Chablis, or Sauvignon Blanc. Be prepared to experiment, though.

## IT'S OKAY TO HAM IT UP WITH HAM

Sometimes, in whatever country you find yourself, if there's any occasion for celebration in progress, certain main dishes invariably show up, just because they're so aesthetically pleasing to the eye and because they just taste so damned good in the bargain. Today's recipe (or variations, thereof), is one of those, as regards ham. Ham, by the way (a word derived from Olde English "ham" or "hon", denoting the hollow or bend of the knee), is a cut of meat from the thigh of an animal, more often than not a pig.

Nearly all of the ham sold, in this present day and age, is fully cooked or cured, and, therefore, can be eaten as-is without additional preparation besides slicing. As an aficionado of ham, as I've undoubtedly mentioned, eating it pretty much exactly as it arrives on my kitchen counter is actually my preference, providing a nice way for me to compare whatever ham I'm eating at the time with whatever ham I've eaten before. In that, there are a wide variety of countries known for their special hams, and each of those hams has a flavor all of its own, harder to distinguish once the meat has been cooked for virtual hours and hours in ingredients that include pineapple, cherries, brown sugar, and even cola.

Countries like Germany, France, China, Croatia, Bulgaria, are famous, respectively, for Westfälischer Schinken from acorn-fed pigs, Bayonne, Jinhau, Prsŭt, and Elenski. While my visits to each of those countries have seen me actively determined to sample each and every ham in its originally processed state, I can't tell you how many times I've been presented at dinners, by locals, with renditions of the following recipe which always look attractive and invariably taste delicious but are far removed from anything pristine from the curing-house.

### Hamming-It-Up Ham

1 (7-10 lb) bone-in ham; **do not use a spiral-cut or it will dry out**
1 lb brown sugar
1 (12-oz) can cola; **not** diet
1 (14-oz) can pineapple slices, drained, reserving juice
1 c Concord-grape wine, such as Manischewitz
10-12 maraschino cherries
Whole cloves (1 small container)

Preheat over to 325°F.

Score ham crosswise and lengthwise, forming a cross-hatch pattern of 1-inch squares about ¼ inch deep. Place a clove in the center of each square.

Place ham, fat side up, on a rack in a roasting pan.

Press sugar on ham. Some sugar will fall off, but use all of the sugar.

Bake until sugar just begins to melt (about 30 minutes).

Remove ham from oven and pour cola all over it. The cola will mix with the brown sugar in the bottom of the pan. Baste ham with the sugar and cola mixture.

Bake for another 30 minutes.

Combine 1 cup of the reserved pineapple juice with the wine. Baste the ham about every 20 minutes with that, as well as the sugar/cola mixture from the bottom of the pan.

Bake about 15-17 minutes per pound, basting every 20 minutes.

Just before the last 20 minutes of baking, remove ham from oven and decorate with pineapple rings, each centered with a cherry, using toothpicks to hold the rings and cherries in place.

Bake for the remaining 20 minutes.

Remove ham from oven.

Let ham rest for at least 25 minutes before removing from pan and transferring to a platter.

Remove fat from pan juices and place juices in pan. Reduce juices, over heat for serving with ham.

**Prior to serving, be sure to remove all toothpicks.**

NOTE: More often than not, I serve this with white Chablis or Sauvignon Blanc. As usual, however, you should experiment to find whatever wine for this pairing is exactly right for you.

# PONDERING THE POTATO

What's wrong with the following paragraph?

> *Septimus Septiminius, member of the Roman Senate, had his reputation to uphold as the best banquet-giver in Roma, and the majority of his guests, the Emperor Trajan included, were inclined to admit that he had certainly outdone himself, this time around, what with his having served up poppy-seed and honey rolls, hot sausages, thrushes stuffed with asparagus, goat and wild-boar pastries, woodcock, flamingo tongues, and a whole Germanic stag served up on a bed of roasted potatoes shipped in specially from far Hibernia...*

The answer of course is that no one in Europe, at the time of Imperial Rome, even residents of Hibernia (present-day Ireland), had ever set eyes on a potato, or several other foods—corn, tomato, bell pepper, chili pepper, vanilla, tobacco, beans, pumpkin, cassava root, avocado, peanut, pecan, cashew, pineapple, blueberry, sunflower, petunia, black-eyed Susan, dahlia, marigold, quinine, cacao (chocolate), gourds, and squash.

Nor would anyone do so in Europe until after Columbus discovered the New World in 1492.

The potato is a native of the Andes Mountains of South America, having evolved at elevations of up to 15,000 feet, where they were first discovered and cultivated by the area's early inhabitants whose archaeological remains, found on the shores of Lake Titicaca, date from 400 BC, although it's estimated the potato, itself, may well have been around for thousands of years before that. Today, in Peru, there's a whole variety of multi-colored potatoes, that never reach our grocery stores, and which, once spotted by me while I was in that country researching my m/m novel BEYOND MACHU and my mainstream novel LOVE'S EMERALD FLAME, had me preparing today's dish, on the spot, just to see how additionally kaleidoscopic I could make it.

I first ate this, though, in Ireland—which didn't adopt the potato as a primary food crop until the 1780s when it was realized that, unlike other crops, potatoes contained most of the vitamins needed to sustain up to ten people on a mere acre of land.

## Potato-Veggie Mélange

½ lb Teeny Tiny New Potatoes [that is what they're called], no bigger than your thumb
2 TBS olive oil
1 TBS butter
1 garlic clove, minced

1 c dried shitake mushrooms, re-hydrated according to package, drained and dried
½ small red onion, thinly sliced
½ lb of small zucchini and yellow squash, sliced
½ lb green beans
Pinch of finely chopped rosemary
Salt and fresh ground pepper, to taste

Boil potatoes until done (about 15 minutes)—do not overcook. Drain, reserving water. Keep potatoes warm.

Heat olive oil and butter over medium heat. Add the garlic and mushrooms. Sauté lightly. Do not stir until they start to brown.

Add the onions. Sauté for another 2 to 3 minutes.

Turn heat to low. Add the zucchini, yellow squash, green beans, and enough of the potato water to cover the bottom of pan.

Sprinkle with pinch of rosemary, salt and pepper.

Cover and stream until squash and green beans are

al-dente tender.

Add potatoes and more potato water if needed, heating through, about 1 minute. Do not drain.

Add more butter or oil, if desired.

Serve immediately.

NOTE: Usually, I pair this dish with Chianti or Pinot Noir.

# CATARACTS, COWBOYS, AND CHATEAUBRIAND

Most people I know, when they're headed to Argentina, end up in Buenos Aires and pretty much stay there. There's something universally appealing about a city as cosmopolitan as this one, with so many fine restaurants, and so many internationally high-end brand-name stores for shopping.

I, on the other hand, have never been all that "into" shopping. While, admittedly, I *am* into fine wining and dining, it's been my experience that, more often than not, the most variety and most interesting meals and wines are found in the hinterlands.

Okay, one of the real reasons behind my seldom remaining long in Buenos Aires before jettisoning it for the countryside is that I have a waterfall fetish... will go (and have gone) thousands of miles out of my way to see a waterfall...and Argentina just happens to have one of world's largest in Iguaçu Falls that was just recently named one of the Seven Natural Wonders of the World; its conglomeration of marvelously wondrous cataracts quickly enticing me to them every time.

After having my fill of Iguaçu, which can take

several days to several weeks, I can never pass up the chance to continue into South America's most renown cattle country to reacquaint myself with the area's cowboys—the gauchos—and yet again, commence with them an overindulgent Marathon of continuous beef-eating, the likes of which I've never even matched in my journeys through the more closer-to-home cow-Mecca known as the U.S.A.'s Great State of Texas.

While I've had one variation or the other of this chapter's recipe, in several countries of the world, I had it first in Argentina, as prepared on an outside grill by a gaucho, at the end of a perfect day on the pampas. At the time, Argentinean meat was so popular, among discerning world meat-eaters, that it was against the law to export, because it had become so expensive for the locals...if they could even find it.

### Argentinean BBQ'd Beef

2 (14-oz) Chateaubriand-cut steaks, about 2" thick
Salt and pepper, to taste
2 c mushroom of choice, sliced
2 garlic cloves, sliced
2 TBS olive oil
2 TBS butter
1½ c beef or veggie stock
1 c burgundy wine

Preheat grill on high.

Oil grill rack.

Salt and pepper steak.

Grill, with cover down, until blood starts to rise on top of steak, about 7 to 10 minutes.

Turn and grill, again, until blood rises on top of steak, about 7 to 10 minutes.

Remove to platter.

Cover and let stand for about 10 to 15 minutes. This is for medium rare; adjust times for rare or well-done.

*While steak is grilling*, sauté mushrooms and garlic in oil *and* butter over medium heat. Do not stir until they start to brown. Remove pan from heat. Add stock and wine. Cook on medium low heat for about 5 minutes. Keep warm, until steak is ready, if necessary.

After steak has rested, carve into slices, about ¼-inch thick. Arrange on platter.

Pour mushrooms and wine sauce over steak.

Serve immediately.

NOTE: Considering I first ate this in Argentina, I usually find myself nostalgically trying to find an Argentinean Malbec to pair with it. Malbec, like Cabernet Sauvignon, has the firm tannins and robustness that can beautifully complement most any well-grilled piece of meat; Argentinean Malbec seldom runs over $25 a bottle. You want to "go-for" a higher-end wine, then try one of the French chateau wines (of which the first-growth Bordeaux, Château Lafite Rothschild always comes first to my mind).

## "SIMPLICITY, THE UTTER SOPHISTICATION"

The title of this section comes from none other than Leonardo da Vinci. There have been others who, in one way or another, pretty much concurred:

> "Everything should be made as simple as possible, but not simpler." ~Albert Einstein.

> "Life is really simple, but we insist on making it complicated." ~Confucius.

> "The wisdom of life consists in the elimination of non-essentials. ~Lin Yutang.

> "How many things are there which I do not want?" ~Socrates

> "Simplicity, simplicity, simplicity!" ~ Henry David Thoreau

The recipe I'm providing next is one of my favorite salads and one of the easiest for you to make. While I know many people who are absolutely scared to death of approaching salad dressings, that often necessitate the seemingly impossible chemistry of actually combining oil and vinegar, believe me when I tell you there is no need to be fearful of doing what has to be done to make this marvelous dish a reality. The irony for me has always been that my first sampling of it occurred when it was presented to me as course fourteen of a twenty-one-course meal. Then again, as anticipated by my French hostess, at the time, most of her guests, by then, were more than ready for something simple, and this salad deliciously fit the bill.

The same friend, over the course of several weeks, during which I ate far simpler fare with her, on a number of different occasions, more than once opted for this salad by way of accompaniment, and I was pleased to see and eat it every time it appeared. To this day, I'm often inclined to prepare it for myself, several days running, especially if fresh baby greens are in season.

### "French Simplicity" Baby Greens Salad

4 to 5 c mixed baby greens
juice of 1 large lemon (approx ¼ c)
½ c olive oil
salt and pepper, to taste
¼ lb thinly shaved Asiago Cheese.

Squeeze lemon into a large bowl.

Slowly whisk in oil.

Add salt and pepper.

Add greens and toss to coat.

Divide onto 4 plates.

Garnish with shaved Asiago Cheese.

NOTE: As I've mentioned before, salads are hard dishes to pair with wines, and it can often take a long time actually, finally, to find the right wine (albeit almost always white) that best suits you and/or your guests. With the acidity of the above's lemon vinaigrette, I inevitably find it safest to serve a Sauvignon Blanc. While I've had guests who have expressed preference for Chardonnay (which often leaves a "buttery" aftertaste), my serving that wine with this salad has never been, and likely never will be, my first choice).

## SCOTCH SCOTCH IF YOU'RE SCOTCH

Once when I was in Las Vegas, U.S.A., I ordered a dram of thirty-six-year old Kinclaith Scotch whisky (and, yes, that is spelled correctly, in that it's English whiskey that has the "e" before the "y"), and it cost me U.S. $450.00.

Once, when in Hong Kong, Special Administrative Region, I ordered an oz of Glenfiddich Scotch whisky, and it cost me U.S. $650.00.

Once, when in Scotland, I was treated to two "fingers" of Scotch whisky in a snifter, which didn't cost me a penny, but which was priceless in that it was from an oak cask, one of only four barreled by a Scottish whisky mogul for each member of his family upon the founding of his distillery over a century before.

Often called just "Scotch", Scotch whisky is a spirit made in Scotland, and aged for at least three years, with a distinct flavor derived from the use of peat (a partially decayed vegetable matter mainly used as a fuel) that's utilized in the roasting of malt during the distilling process.

Those people who are not Scotch whisky aficionados, even those accustomed to the large bankrolls required, these days, to purchase a premium bottle of vintage French wine, often are mind-blown to discover that a bottle of Scotch whisky, single-malt, aged for fifty or more years, can, and has, sold in excess of U.S.$80,000.00.

That is why, likewise as regards pricy wines, I always tell everyone to forego "the expensive", especially as far as Scotch whisky in cooking. Much of the alcohol used in recipes is burned off by the heat; really good booze is really put to best advantage by merely drinking it.

For cooking, you can pick up a bottle of plain whiskey (with the "e" before the "y"), for less than U.S. $50.00, and it'll serve your purposes just fine in the following recipe which I first ate on the edge of a Scottish moor, a bagpipe forlornly playing in the background as wisps of ghostly fog literally danced in from the heath to join me and others in a truly macabre *Macbeth*—"When shall we three meet again...?"—moment.

### Whiskey Steak Sandwich

½ c soy sauce
½ c teriyaki sauce
¼ c Worcestershire sauce
¼ c whiskey
¼ c brown sugar
¾ c red onion, finely chopped
2 TBS garlic, chopped
1 TBS olive oil

1 tsp dry mustard
Kosher salt
black pepper, freshly ground
4-8 oz flank steak, London broil, or sirloin, about 1- to 1½-inch thick
6 six-inch rolls, such as Italian or Kaiser, split
½ c butter, softened
1 tsp Italian parsley, finely chopped
2 large tomatoes, sliced
6 (or more) slices fresh mozzarella cheese or sliced cheddar

Marinade:

Combine the soy sauce, teriyaki sauce, Worcestershire sauce, whiskey, brown sugar, onion, 1 TBS chopped garlic, olive oil, dry mustard, pinch of salt, and a pinch of pepper in a sealable plastic food bag. Add steaks: marinate for at least one hour, up to overnight, turning occasionally.

Preheat grill to high.

Just before serving, combine butter, remaining 1 TBS chopped garlic, the parsley, a pinch of salt and pepper. Spread mixture on the split side of rolls. Set aside.

Turn grill to medium.

Remove steaks from marinade; discard marinade.

Grill steaks over direct heat for about 8–10 minutes, depending on the thickness of steak (about 160°F for medium-well). Do not overcook.

Remove from grill, cover. Let stand for about 5 minutes.

As steaks are resting, lightly brown rolls over medium heat on the grill, 1 to 2 minutes.

Thinly slice steaks across the grain, diagonally. Divide between the rolls.

Top with sliced tomatoes and cheese slices. If desired, return to grill, but not over direct heat, for 1 to 2 minutes to melt cheese.

Top with roll tops. Cut in half and serve immediately.

Makes 6 big sandwiches.

NOTE: While I often pair this sandwich with shots of whiskey (with the "e"—whisky without the "e" saved just for drinking on its own), I've discovered, for those who prefer wine with their meals, that a Cabernet Sauvignon or Merlot often serves the purpose.

# WHEN GIVEN A LEMON IN LIFE...MAKE LEMONADE, OR...

Conceding to the prevalent belief that lemons, reported hybrids from a sour orange and a citron, first grew in southern India, northern Burma, and in China, there's no denying that a couple of my very fond memories of that fruit revolve around having encountered it in Saudi Arabia. Not altogether unfitting, I guess, in that the lemon was apparently first mentioned in a tenth-century Arabic treatise on farming and has, for a very long time, been used as an "ornamental" in Islamic gardens.

I was incoming from a two-day jaunt into the *Rub' al Khali* (Empty Quarter) of the Arabian Peninsula (I have this "thing" for deserts or waterfalls that will have me go thousands of miles out of my way to see either one), when we stopped at a wayside rest station among an orchard of lemon trees whose greenery was some of the first we'd spotted after officially exiting the largest sand desert in the world.

I watched while lemons were plucked from their tree, sliced, squeezed, mixed with sugar and water, with the addition of seemingly rarer-than-diamonds-at-the-time ice, to be served up as one of the most refreshing and memorable quaffs I've ever had the pleasure of drinking in my entire lifetime.

While in Najran, one of the most interesting but least-visited Arabian oasis cities, on the Yemeni border, once a caravan stop on the spice route, and inhabited for 4000 years, I, early one morning, accompanied my host as he beheaded a chicken, plucked it, butchered it, marinated it in olive oil infused with fresh Rosemary harvested from his garden, and added the juice of one very fresh lemon picked directly from his decidedly beautiful but very lone lemon tree. The resulting grilled dish that he served up later that evening is one I've been trying to duplicate for a very long time.

Even with the help of Bonnie Clark, my co-author, of *BACK OF THE BOAT GOURMET COOKING* and *EVEN GOURMANDS HAVE TO DIET*, and helpmate in this memoir, I've been unable quite to match the exceptional deliciousness I remember from that one particularly spectacular Arabian evening; although, the following recipe comes about as close as I think I'm ever going to get without heading back to Arabia for another lemon from that one exceptionally beautiful lone lemon tree.

## Arabian-Grilled Rosemary-Lemon Chicken

juice of 1 lemon, about ⅓ c
¼ c olive oil
a pinch of fresh Rosemary, finely chopped
salt and pepper to taste
2 whole chicken breasts, skinless and boneless

Mix the lemon juice, olive oil, rosemary, salt and pepper in a lockable plastic food bag.

Butterfly the chicken and put in the bag. Close tightly and "smoosh" around to coat completely.

Refrigerate for a minimum of 20 minutes, up to 24 hours.

Preheat grill on high. Turn down to medium.

Grill chicken for about 3 minutes.

Turn and grill for another 3 minutes.

Remove to platter; cover and let sit for about 5 to 10 minutes.

Slice and serve immediately over following mixed baby greens salad:

4 to 5 c of mixed baby greens
juice of 1 large lemon, about ¼ c
½ c olive oil

salt and pepper, to taste
4 TBS dried cranberries
4 tsp chopped pecans

Squeeze lemon into a large bowl.

Slowly whisk in oil.

Add salt and pepper.

Add greens and toss to coat.

Divide onto 4 plates.

Garnish with dried cranberries and pecans.

Serves 4.

NOTE: Yes, I have been known to serve this with lemonade from freshly squeezed lemons. If not, I invariably rely upon a white wine from eastern Idaho State, U.S.A., Ste. Chapelle Soft White, which has just enough sweetness to cut the acidity of the lemon, without being so sweet as to overpower the dish.

# SURF'S UP...
# FORMALITY ISN'T

It wasn't so surprising that the meal was easily prepared. Surfers are far better known for "hanging ten" than for serving up ten-course meals. My companions and I, for that long weekend, were surfers.

It might well have been surprising, and may still be, to those who aren't acquainted with surfing beyond the beaches of Hawaii, and California, U.S.A., or Australia, to learn that we were just outside Busan, South Korea, on Haeundae Beach at the time. That said...most people familiar with the surfing world, as I am, know that waves are found wherever in the world waves are found, and South Korea, under the right conditions, can supply more than adequate surf to make riding them worth the time and effort expended to get there.

Most surprising to me and to anyone else, though, might well be that my group of surfers, in South Korea, was eating burritos, a menu item certainly more indicative of northern Mexico than of the Orient, courtesy not of any local Asian market, with a mysterious and uncharacteristic cache of tortilla shells, and jarred salsa, but because one of our group had access to the Post Exchange (PX) of the South Korean U.S. Army installation to which he was assigned for active duty. As luck would have it, that PX's Supply Sergeant, of Tex-Mex ancestry, long having missed any semblance of "home-made" to the tacos, burritos, or enchiladas served up in the Army Mess Hall, had ordered enough tortilla shells and jarred salsa to satisfy his own independent needs with some left over for the rest of those on base with access to the PX's grocery store.

Since that night, on that South Korean beach, I've called the following recipe after that Oriental location where I most often remember eating it. By way of burritos, though, these are pretty standard fare, found just about anywhere that burritos are prepared, and called by any number of names; but I'll likely continue to call them what I call them.

Their advantage, aside from the memories they recall for me, is that they're pretty simple to prepare, nothing fancy needed, especially if you've saved some of the chicken you had from your meal of the night before, like we did—as well as any jarred salsa from your local grocery store, as well as tortillas easily warmed on the heated stones of a beach campfire.

When, at home, these days, I usually supplement with the cheese, lettuce, sour cream, jalapeños, and the chopped fresh tomatoes I've mentioned below; you should feel free to add or subtract at your discretion.

## Busan (Chicken) Beach Burritos

2 whole wheat tortillas
left-over pre-cooked chicken (shredding provides a nice touch)
salsa (home-made is always good, although, for simplicity, any bottled version will do).

Heat tortilla shells until warm.

Layer each warm tortilla shell with left-over pre-cooked chicken.

Pour on salsa to taste.

Roll contents up within the containing tortilla shells.

Cut, for convenience, if desired.

Eat.

As a quick aside: if you've a pan handy, you can combine the left-over pre-cooked chicken with the salsa (and a bit of water, if more moisture is needed), then heat that before layering it on your tortilla shells.

Likewise, if desired, before rolling your tortilla shells—

Include as chief ingredients, or as side dishes, or as garnishes:

cheese
lettuce
sour cream
tomatoes
jalapeños
guacamole

and/or whatever else might catch your fancy.

NOTE: I usually skip all formal wine pairings with this dish and serve it with cold beer. In South Korea, it was usually from the Hite Brewing Company that sells various brands. Wherever you are, though, just grab up some of the local brewskie, preferably get it ice-cold... and Cowabunga!

# BEYOND BOOKS... BERLIN, AND BEER

There are some drinks and foods which simply should be, just for the fun of it, imbibed or eaten at specific places on the globe, should you ever be there, despite any obvious clichés, just so you can actually say, "Been there. Done that. Got the T-shirt. Burned it. Tossed the ashes." I'm talking Singapore Sling cocktails at Raffles Hotel in Singapore, Southeast Asia...Frankfurters in Frankfurt, Germany...Devonshire Cream in Devon, U.K...Baked Alaska in Alaska, U.S.A...Swedish Meatballs in Sweden...Yorkshire Pudding in Yorkshire, U.K...Sardines in Sardinia... Scotch in Scotland, U.K....

I'm talking Hamburgers in Hamburg, Germany, like the one I remember served up to me, there, by a dear family friend after I had been asked by her if there was anything in particular that I'd like to eat while visiting.

Having had several of my books go German-language editions, via a couple of mainstream German publishers, I've a budding relationship with people in the German publishing industry, as well as a fan base, all of which gives me the good excuse to include

Deutschland in any of my planned European itineraries. Initially, I pretty much stayed centered in Berlin, drinking German beers, usually during Oktoberfest. Later, though, once I'd pretty much "seen" the capital city, I expanded my sightseeing horizons, especially as my parents had a long-time friend in Hamburg to whom they'd always hoped I'd stop by to say an up-close-and-personal hello.

Okay, admittedly, there are some existing culinary arguments ongoing as to whether or not the hamburger was actually invented in Hamburg, Germany (probably not). Many results of valid research actually attribute it, in its present ground-beef-paddy-between-two-slices-of-a-halved-bun to the U.S.A.; the Hamburg, Germany, connection likely merely referring to early German immigrants to the U.S.A. having had a decided penchant for conveniently prepared and easily eaten ground beef. So, if my U.S.A. readers prefer to eat your hamburger in Hamburg, New York, U.S.A. (or your London Broil in London, New York, U.S.A.), that's certainly you're prerogative—and a whole lot cheaper than my proffered European alternatives. It's all just kind of a game to which everyone can make his or her own rules by way of playing.

## Hamburg Hamburger

Onion Straws (See recipe in my book, co-authored by Bonnie Clark, *BACK OF THE BOAT GOURMET COOKING: AFLOAT—POOL-SIDE—BACKYARD*, available everywhere.)
1½ lb ground meat (beef, elk, buffalo...whatever)
1 jalapeño pepper, seeded and finely diced
Salt and pepper to taste
4 slices cheese (cheddar, Swiss, pepper jack...whatever)
4 round halved buns (preferably "hoagies", but you can even use 8 bread slices if you prefer)
Cream cheese
8 slices bacon, cooked crisp
1 ripe avocado, sliced
1 tomato, ¼-inch slices
Lettuce

Make Onion Straws, according to the recipe. (Probably will make a lot more than you need; if you don't, they'll most likely all be eaten before the burgers are even ready).

Mix the ground meat with the diced jalapeño pepper, and divide into 4 patties.

Salt and pepper to taste.

Grill, broil, or fry all of the paddies, turning them once.

Top with cheese, and continue cooking to the desired

doneness.

Toast the cut sides of the halved buns. Spread all the toasted halves with the cream cheese.

Spatula-deliver a hamburger paddy to each of four toasted bun halves.

Top each hamburger paddy with two slices of bacon, as well as a slice of avocado and tomato. Add some lettuce, and, then, pile on Onion Straws.

Place remaining bun halves on the tops of their corresponding companion pieces.

Makes 4 large servings.

NOTE: If you're into beer, especially German beer, here's the opportunity to serve a pale lager, Holsten Pilsener, if just because the Holsten Brewery is located in Hamburg, Germany. Admittedly, though, I experienced my best meal of beef hamburger when it was teamed up with a very expensive vintage French Bordeaux. When and if selecting a wine, though, be sure to remember that your preferences may change depending upon what kind of meat you're using; you may enjoy a Zinfandel with beef, a Shiraz with lamb, or a Pinot Noir with turkey....

# TOTO, I DON'T THINK WE'RE IN KANSAS ANYMORE

"Shrimps on the barbie!"

I couldn't help but laugh at that announcement, as playfully shouted across the patio by my Australian host, because it was intentionally so stereotypically reminiscent of a whole series of commercials aired on U.S.A. television between 1984-1990, compliments of the Australian Tourism Commission, and starring Paul Hogan (of the then-popular "Crocodile Dundee" franchise; although, it's my understanding that the ads were actually shot before Hogan became so famous). "Barbie", of course, is Australian slang for barbecue. "Shrimp", though exactly what my Australian host was preparing in my honor that evening, was actually a misnomer of the U.S.A ad campaign, used only because most North Americans can't tell the difference between a shrimp and a prawn, (there IS a difference), and have a tendency to call both shrimp. Actually, prawns are what the Aussies prefer and usually eat, often at Christmastime, although my host had gone out of his way to find shrimp, just for me.

The "Oz" location of my shrimps-on-the-barbie moment was, likewise, reminiscent of at least one of the Hogan commercials, in that it was (and still is) a beautiful estate adjacent to Sydney Harbor. The panorama affords aesthetically pleasant viewing of what a lot of people consider the world's most beautiful port, and includes the Sydney skyline, the Sydney Harbor Bridge, and the Sydney Opera house whose famed sail-like construction seemingly mirrors those of the myriad yachts usually found on the water in summer.

It was all very civilized and pretty much in direct contrast to my activities of the preceding lead-in days and nights. By way of researching my Aussie m/m book, *SNAKES*, and my m/f novel *DARE TO LOVE IN OZ*, I'd been trekking the Australian bush...getting dirty, dusty, mining for opals (I ended up with two), climbing Ayres Rock, seeing five of the world's top-ten most poisonous snakes, scouring the deep-outback for its isolated ancient petroglyphs, dining on fresh kangaroo steaks prepared over open campfires, and enduring a day-long sandstorm. The latter was even worse than the one I encountered in the Sahara that saw me head-covered and hunkered down beside my shielding camel. Though the Oz sandblasting had us sheltering in a convenient cave, it's interesting that I did see several of the feral camels still roaming the Australian wilderness as a result of their ancestors having been imported to Oz in the nineteenth-century for use as transport in the colonization of the area.

## Wizard of Oz Shrimp and Pasta

1 lb large shrimp, peeled and de-veined
Olive oil
Salt and pepper
1-lb package spaghetti
½ c onions, diced
3 cloves of garlic, finely diced
6 Crimini mushrooms, roughly chopped
¼ c olive oil
⅓ c balsamic vinegar
1½ TBS Dijon mustard
3 Roma tomatoes, seeded and roughly chopped
10 basil leaves, chopped
Salt and pepper, freshly ground (to taste)

Divide shrimp on skewers. Do not crowd. Place on plate or shallow pan. Drizzle with olive oil and salt and pepper. Refrigerate until ready to grill.

While preparing the pasta, following directions on the package, until al dente....

Preheat grill on high.

Oil the grate.

In a large pan, sauté onions, garlic, and mushrooms in ¼ c olive oil, about 3-5 minutes.

Add vinegar and mustard. Cook 5 minutes more.

Turn grill to medium.

Place skewers over direct heat. Cook shrimp until pink, about 2-3 minutes on each side.

Drain the pasta. Toss with the onion mixture. Add tomatoes, basil and salt and pepper to taste; toss lightly. Top with shrimp and serve.

Serves 4.

NOTE: I know it's pretty much *de rigueur* to recommend a white wine for seafood dishes, especially since the last book in my *WILLIAM MALTESE'S WINE TASTER'S DIARY* series is all about an Australian white—*IN SEARCH OF THE PERFECT PINOT G! AUSTRALIA'S MORNINGTON PENINSULA* (written with A. B. Gayle)—but my Australian host, as well as I (then, and since), have found this dish really too rich for too many genuinely successful white-wine pairings. On the evening in question, by way of a red, it went well with an Australian Parri Estate Winery Cabernet Sauvignon. Since then, I've had success by accompanying it with (the reds) Zinfandel or Merlot.

# GOBBLER, GOBBLE...
# BANG! GOBBLE

My diet isn't exclusively non-gluten even if I enjoy non-gluten and have co-authored a book with Adrienne Z. Milligan about it—*THE GLUTEN-FREE WAY: MY WAY*. The book was actually inspired by the necessity of my co-author, and her family, to go on an entirely gluten-free regimen.

My diet isn't exclusively vegan even if I enjoy vegan, have a vegan cake—"William Maltese Spice Cake"—named after me, and I've co-authored a vegan dessert book—*GET-REAL VEGAN DESSERTS: VEGAN RECIPES FOR THE REST OF US*. The book was actually inspired by my co-author, Christina-Marie "Sexy Vegan Mama" Wright, who refuses to dine on anything with a face.

My eating habits are pretty much based upon an eclectic try-anything-once mentality. If and when confronted with anything edible, even if new and unusual, in my extensive world travels, I've inevitably stepped right up, food utensil in hand (if needed), and have proceeded to chow down—whether on tarantula in Cambodia, monkey brains in Singapore, durian in Malaysia, bat soup in Thailand, fugu in Japan, or whatever.

Certainly, I've never shied from meat. In fact, I can't really imagine my diet without it. Nor have I, whenever the opportunity has presented itself, missed out on a chance to play provider and actually hunt the meat that I eat—whether that be boar in Korea, kangaroo in Australia, giraffe in Africa, caribou in Alaska, or peacock in New Zealand.

That brings me to my hunting wild turkey in the State of Georgia, U.S.A., and a recipe which is particularly "Georgian" if for no other reason than the recipe calls for a marinade made with Sprite® soft drink which is a product of the Coca-Cola® company headquartered in Atlanta, Georgia, U.S.A.

Although a lot of people in the U.S.A. think that the only turkey available to them is the domesticated variety found plastic-wrapped in their local grocery stores...under the misconception that wild turkey somehow became extinct with the Pilgrims...the fact remains that Georgia is a great place still to hunt the eastern wild turkey, with that fowl's largest population in the U.S.A., and the longest (almost 2-month) hunting season. Some mature Georgian gobblers weigh 18-24 pounds, and there's a 90% success rate for shooters participating in organized hunts.

# Georgian-Sprite® Wild Turkey Breasts

2 c. Sprite® soft drink
1 c. soy sauce
¼ c. oil
½ tsp wasabi horseradish
5 lb of boneless wild turkey breasts (domesticated turkey breasts may be substituted)

For marinade, whisk together the Sprite®, soy sauce, oil, and the wasabi horseradish.

Put turkey breasts in a plastic food-storage bag. Pour marinade over turkey, making sure the turkey is covered with the marinade. Seal bag. Refrigerate for at least 8 hours; the longer the better, occasionally turning the bag to make sure the turkey is evenly exposed to the marinade.

Preheat grill on high.

Oil grate.

Turn grill to medium-high.

Place turkey breasts on grill.

Cover turkey breasts loosely with a piece of foil.

Baste turkey often, turning until cooked and/or juices run clear (about 10 minutes on each side—don't overcook).

Remove turkey from grill; cover with foil and let sit for about 10 minutes.

Slice and serve over rice, quinoa noodles, or green salad.

For a sauce, put 1 cup Sprite® and 1 cup soy sauce in a sauce pan over medium-high. Reduce liquid about ⅓. Add 1 TBS of butter. Stir. Once butter is melted, spoon the resulting sauce over the turkey and/or dip the turkey in it.

Serves 8-10.

NOTE: Because of the sweet/saltiness of its marinade, this dish is one I've successfully paired with Pinot Noir (red), as well as with always-popular Chardonnay (white).

# GOOD GRUB WITHOUT GALLIVANTING

Pretty much like regular meatballs, it can be made of ground beef, lamb, pork, veal, venison, poultry, or any combination thereof. It can include vegetables, even a hard-boiled egg. In Austria, it's called *Faschierter Braten*; in Bulgaria, Руло Стефани; in Finland, *lihamureke*; in Germany, *Faschierter Braten*; in Greece, Ρολό; in Hungary, *Stefánia szelet*; in Italy, *polpettone*; in the Philippines, *embotido*; in Romania, *drob*.

I pretty much always refer to it just as "meatloaf", because that's what it's called in the U.S. of A. While I've eaten it in all of the above versions, in all of the above countries, this is one of those dishes, like my "Aunt Dorthy's Salad" (mentioned in this book's "Family Jewels" chapter), that sees me having found one of my favorite recipes for it close to home.

A version of meatloaf, using minced meat, is mentioned as early as the fourth-to-fifth century in the Roman epicurean collection titled *De Re Coquinaria* ("On the Subject of Cooking"), usually attributed to Caelius Apicius. The American equivalent is rumored to have made its debut via a mixture of ground pork and corn meal, known as "scrapple", served by the Pennsylvania Dutch (actually Germans and/or Swiss) in U.S. colonial times, but there's seemingly no official mention of it in U.S. cookbooks until the late 1800s.

Inevitably eaten with sauce or relish, the former... often made from tomatoes...is usually poured over the uncooked loaf to form a crust during baking; although many diners resort to merely shaking on ketchup at the table. Some versions substitute simple (more often than not, onion) brown gravy, barbecue sauces (of one kind or another), mustard, or merely a drizzling of melted butter. One variation actually cooks the loaf covered in mashed potatoes.

My favorite way of eating it is as a leftover, cold, thick-sliced, and made into a sandwich, with a liberal slathering of home-made horseradish between hearty slices of rye bread.

### Auntie May's Meatloaf

3 slices bread
1 small can canned milk
1½ lb ground turkey, chicken, or beef
14 oz can diced tomatoes
½ c green pepper, chopped
6 medium cremini mushrooms, roughly chopped
1 large onion, chopped
3 eggs, slightly beaten
Ketchup

Preheat oven to 400°F.

Grease or spray a cookie-sheet-like low-sided 10-x-13-inch pan, and set aside.

Tear bread into chunks. Cover with milk and let stand.

Put meat, tomatoes, pepper, mushrooms, onion, and eggs into a bowl. Add bread and milk. Mix with hands, lightly but thoroughly.

Spread in pan about 1½-inch high, staying about 1½-inch from sides of pan.

Spread ketchup over top to cover.

Bake for 1 hour.

Serves approximately 8.

NOTE: Often still considered a North American "peasant/comfort food", because of early preparations using ground-up leftover meats, this dish can pretty much be paired with just about any red wine that's your particular favorite; I've had my best successes with medium-bodied Cabernet Sauvignons, spicy Merlots, or the usually always food-friendly Zinfandels.

# BEER, BEER...
# HERE, HERE!

For anyone who hasn't been to Germany for Oktoberfest, I can't recommend it highly enough. It's one of those experiences not to be missed...like La Tomatina in Spain, the Alba White Truffle Fair in Italy, the Galway Oyster Festival in Ireland, the Baltic Herring Festival in Finland, The Salon du Chocolate in France, and the Gilroy Garlic Festival in California, USA.

Don't make the big mistake, though, of going to Germany for Oktoberfest in October, or you'll miss most of the fun. Paradoxically, the festivity begins in the middle of September and is pretty much into close-down mode by the time its namesake month of October actually rolls around. All of which is the result of a conscious effort by the hosting nation to assure the event, and the massive influx of locals and tourists who attend, can advantage the last of the German summer warmth and sunshine.

This is the largest festival in the world, with over six million visitors annually, and it's celebrated nationwide, although the primary events take place in the city of Munich. In whatever German city you happen to find yourself at the time, be advised that you should make reservations for seats, every day, in whatever your preferred beer-house "pavilion", because all available space can fill quickly, without an empty chair in sight by nightfall. Certainly, don't drive, not just because drinking and driving is never to be recommended, but because parking is next to impossible. You're far better off joining the crowds cramming public transport, because that, at least, pretty much assures you'll get where you're going, along with everyone else who'll likely be headed in the same direction as you are.

While beer is certainly the star of the occasion, there's no way that you're likely to avoid the whole panoply of German cuisine that's made available as well. And while I've spent more than one Oktoberfest pigging out on traditional fare, like *currywurst*, fried potatoes, obazda, potato pancakes, potato salad, pretzels, sautéed mushrooms, and *wurstsalat*, my recipe, this time around, came to me by way of one very drunken night, during Oktoberfest, in Munich, in a tent sponsored by some brewery or restaurant (I can't really remember which). I was so impressed, though, by my order of fried-steak snacks, served up with my humongous stein of beer, that I insisted upon summoning the cook responsible who good-naturedly (probably wanting to avoid a scene with a drunken American) wrote out the recipe for me on the back of some beer-stained butcher paper. For which I, over the years, continue to be grateful.

## Oktoberfest "Munich" Steak Fingers

for Part #1:

2 lb steak (any inexpensive cut will do...aka round, flank, sirloin tip...)
3 cloves garlic, finely diced
2 TBS "William Maltese Hottie Spice Mix" [or YOUR favorite spice mix—the former (named after me, after all) available on-line and on-site through The Heart of Spokane, in Spokane WA USA.]
2 tsps Kosher Salt
1 tsp sugar
1 tsp pepper, freshly ground
2 tsp onion powder
1 tsp paprika
¼ c olive oil
¼ c red wine (burgundy as good a choice as any)

for Part #2:

1½ c of all-purpose flour
2 tsp garlic salt
1 tsp pepper, freshly ground
Cooking oil (your preference) for frying

Part #1:

Cut steak into ½-inch strips, about 2-3 inches long. Place steaks in a large re-sealable plastic food-storage bag.

Combine the garlic, spice mix, Kosher salt, sugar, ground pepper, onion powder, and paprika in a bowl. Whisk in the oil and wine. Pour over the steak in the bag and seal the bag.

Refrigerate at least 6 hours, preferably overnight.

Part #2:

Just before frying, combine flour, garlic salt, and ground pepper in a bowl. Coat steak strips, a few at a time. Be sure NOT to overcrowd in pan, and fry in oil until steak is brown on all sides or cooked through. (Steak may, also, be deep-fried).

Serve with your favorite sauce or dip.

Serves 4 to 6.

NOTE: Of course, I usually serve beer, German beer, at that, whenever I bring out these delicious snacks, and I recommend you do the same. If you likely won't be able to find any of the special, darker, and stronger, Oktoberfest beer (*Wiesn Märzen*), specifically brewed for the occasion, feel free to substitute Spaten, Paulaner, and/or Hofbräu. Hell, even most (albeit watered-down) American brews will suffice, in a pinch. And for those of your guests who simply can't bring themselves to drink anything BUT wine, try serving them a Sauvignon Blanc or Muscadet.

# TIME FOR BEANY!

*Time for Beany* was a puppet-dominated television show, originating from Los Angeles, U.S.A., that broadcasted roughly from 1949-1955. Each episode lasted fifteen minutes and portrayed the ongoing adventures of a precocious young seaman, Beany, who wore his trademark beanie cap, as he sailed the high seas on the ship "Leakin' Lena". Along with him was a brave but none-too-bright 300-year-old, thirty-five-foot Seasick Sea Serpent by the name of Cecil, a stubborn "Uncle Captain" Horatio Huffenpuff, and the villain, Dishonest John (complete with cape and handlebar mustache). The group was rounded out by a dotted lion, named Tearalong and a circus clown, Clownie; the latter an early cast drop-out.

The show became well-known for its satire that, more often than not, spoofed celebrities of the time, like President Truman, Red Skeleton, and Dinah Shore, and came to be enjoyed not only by children but by adults as well. Among the later were Frank Zappa, Harpo Marx, and even the august Albert Einstein, who is rumored to have interrupted a longer-than-he bargained-for meeting by excusing himself to go see a scheduled *Time for Beany* episode.

My green-bean recipe that follows...besides being another indication that gourmands, like I, are often inclined to get fat, and, therefore, do, on occasions, make the wise decision of opting for single-vegetable dishes, rather than eight-course meals...comes to you, in a roundabout manner, from a Hollywood dinner party once hosted by Robert "Bob" Emerson Clampett who was the American animator responsible for creating the *Time for Beany* series.

Impressed by Bob's (or by his cook's?) take on a classical Italian green-bean menu selection, two of his Italian guests, at the meal, asked for, and were given, the U.S.A. recipe to take cross-Atlantic with them to their Italian city, Gabbioneta-Binanuova, in Italy's Cremonia Province, Lombardy. This is where, years later, I happened upon it after consenting to my hostess's invitation to join her in a light "Time for Beany" lunch, featuring some of the fresh green beans picked, just that morning, from her very own garden.

## "Beany" Green-Beans

Part #1:

Make some Classic Basil Pesto [the below recipe comes to you compliments of my *BACK OF THE BOAT GOURMET COOKING* book (available everywhere), written with Bonnie Clark]—

3 TBS pine nuts
2 c basil, fresh leaves, firmly packed
½ c olive oil
½ tsp garlic, minced
Salt (hopefully Napa-style, coarse, gray), to taste
A pinch of Ascorbic Acid, or Vitamin-C powder
¼ c freshly grated Parmesan cheese

Place pine nuts in a dry pan, over medium heat. Keep the pan moving, and cook until nuts start to brown.

Set pan and nuts to one side to cool.

Prepare a bowl of ice water.

Put basil in a sieve or strainer and place in a pot of boiling water. (NOTE: be sure the leaves are completely covered with liquid).

Stir boiling basil about 15 seconds, and, then, plunge into your bowl of ice-cold water to cool them quickly.

Immediately drain the water from the basil and squeeze from the leaves any residual liquid.

Roughly chop the basil.

Puree the basil with the toasted pine nuts, the olive oil, garlic, salt, and pinch of the powdered Ascorbic Acid, in a blender. (NOTE: a blender does a better job of this than does a food processor).

When blended, add the cheese until well-mixed.

Makes about ¾ cup.

Keep refrigerated before use.

NOTE: I make as many batches of this as I can from any available fresh basil I have on hand, on any one time, and, then, I freeze it. Sometimes with a bumper crop of basil, I'll have enough pesto to last me through the winter. Basil is easily grown, whether in the garden, or in pots inside. It likes hot weather, and it'll die at the first sign of frost—so be forewarned. By the way, Ascorbic Acid or Vitamin C keeps the pesto from turning brown and provides a slight enjoyable citric flavor. You can get Ascorbic Acid in powdered form at any health-food store. Sometimes, though, I just buy Vitamin-C tablets, wherever those are sold, and use a mortar and pestle to powder the pills for whatever the pinch or two that's required.

Part #2:

2 c fresh green beans
Salt and pepper to taste
2 TBS Classic Basil Pesto (See Part #1)
1 TBS extra-virgin olive oil
1 TBS freshly grated Parmesan cheese

In a large pot with a steamer basket, add enough water to just about touch the bottom of the basket. Bring to a boil. Put beans into the basket and turn the heat to simmer. Keep at simmer and cook beans about 5 to 8 minutes, until the desired doneness.

In the meantime, heat the oil and the prepared basil pesto in a pan over low heat.

Drain beans.

Salt and pepper the beans, then add the heated oil and pesto, making sure to coat the beans thoroughly.

Put beans in a serving dish and sprinkle with freshly grated Parmesan cheese

Serve immediately.

Serves 4 to 5.

NOTE: The wine you pair with this will depend upon whether you're serving the beans as a light meal, all on their own, or using them as a side dish with something else by way of a main course. In Italy, as a light lunch, we enjoyed these with a bottle of Sicilian Bianco di Caselle. Since I've found that wine, though, hard to come by, except in Sicily, try any Sauvignon Blanc. If you've prepared this as a side dish, of course, choose whatever wine that best complements your main course.

# SAUCY APPLE-OF-MY-EYE

Whether I'm in the northern or the southern hemisphere, cold weather suddenly on its way, I invariably have the uncontrollable inclination to fly out with the next flock of birds smart enough to be heading for warmer climes.

Occasionally, I find myself willing to stay put within the confining (for me) parameters of a Mother-Nature-induced chill. For example, cold weather is a good time for me to stay indoors, at the computer, if I'm kept warm by a roaring fire, as well as by imbibing hot toddies and hot-buttered rums, in that I can expect (hopefully), at least until I get drunk, to get lots of writing done.

Then, ever so often (less so than before), I get the crazy inclination to climb some mountain—like Mt. Rainier in Washington State USA, or Mt. Kilimanjaro, Tanzania—which has perpetual snow and ice on its summit. As well, I'm always figuring that I really should, far more often, use my expensive ski clothing and gear in order to consider those major expenditures worthwhile; although, I usually end up doing more partying in warm lodges and in friends' heated chalets than I do chilling out on slippery slopes.

Finally, I've been known to advantage the wondrously kaleidoscopic coloring of all the leaves on all the deciduous trees found in Vermont State in the U.S. of A. when autumn's cold weather sets in there. The area is so well-known for its preponderance of varied and vibrant leaf colors that there are yearly Fall-Foliage tours conducted, during which people flock to the area specifically to marvel at Nature's brilliance in painting a seemingly never-ending landscape with such exceedingly natural, albeit transitory, brilliance.

Admittedly, though, as far as I'm concerned, it's not just the pretty leaves that draw me to Vermont but the State's apples as well...and a way those apples (Macintosh in particular) can be combined with another Vermont specialty, maple syrup, into a decidedly tasty treat that was first my pleasure to enjoy when served to me by a favorite Bed-and-Breakfast proprietor, since deceased, always remembered fondly by me whenever I prepare the dish in question.

Unlike Vermont's apples, its maple syrup (yes, by the way, from maple trees, needing approximately forty to fifty gallons of sap to boil down to make one gallon of syrup), isn't harvested at the end of summer but in the late winter and/or early spring. Therefore, tourists out for the wondrous leaves and tasty apples miss out on the tapping of the maple trees; but, as of late, I personally judge that no big deal, in that the one-time rustic charm of quaint spouts and individual buckets used to gather sap, has been replaced by unsightly runs of plastic tubing from tree to tree. That said, Vermont maple syrup is available year-round, often in convenient plastic jugs, making it always readily accessible for cooking.

Maple syrup, in the United States, is divided into two major grades—A and B—corresponding to the part of the season in which the syrup is produced. Grade A, light amber in color, is an early-season syrup; Grade B, darker in color, is late-season and usually less sweet, and even thought by some to come across slightly medicinal. Grade B, as in this recipe, is what's most often used in cooking and baking.

### Vermont Applesauce

4 to 5 lb apples, Macintosh...or Gala, or Gravenstein...
Juice of 1 lemon (about 3 TBS)
¼ c butter
½ tsp salt
Pinch of pepper
⅓ c maple syrup, Grade B

Preheat oven to 425°F.

Peel, core, and, then, cut apples into 1-inch pieces and put in bowl.

Squeeze lemon over apples pieces and toss to coat.

Melt butter over medium-high heat in a large, ovenproof sauté pan, until butter starts to brown.

Add apples, salt and pepper.

Sauté until apples just start to brown (3 or 4 minutes).

Add Grade-B maple syrup, stirring to coat apples.

Put in oven for about 20 to 30 minutes until apples are lightly caramelized and soft.

Remove from oven.

For chunky applesauce, mash with fork; for smoother sauce, put apples in food processor or blender.

Serves 8.

NOTE: As with my previous green beans recipe, pairing this applesauce with wine depends upon whether or not you serve it on its own as a snack, or as a side dish (it's delicious as an accompaniment for pork). The former has seen me enjoying Toso Moscato Dolce, a charming Italian Sparkling Wine, reminiscent of honeysuckle and rose petals. The latter, especially if your pork is barbecued, can include pretty much the whole range of medium-bodied reds from Tempranilloto to Zinfandel.

# NO NEED TO "CHUCK" IT

I can personally avouch that the chuck wagon—that portable kitchen on wooden-wagon wheels that was such a major part of the U.S.A.'s early Westward-Ho expansion movement—is still, on occasion, alive and well today, and at the disposal of cowboy cooks feeding twenty-first-century ranch hands in out-of-the-way sections of wind-swept North American landscapes.

I knew this icon from early western days to be, in fact, a long-lasting survivor, when I spent some time on a working ranch, some time back, doing research for my novels *BUCK*...and *TIED-UP RANCH HANDS*...and *MONTANA BOUND*. I reconfirmed it more recently, though, while writing my latest western novel, *RIDE THE MAN DOWN*...after having heard that all chuck wagons were quickly being replaced by four-wheel drive all-terrain vehicles, with the resulting tailgate feedings of present-day cow- and horse-herding cowboys out on the range.

While, yes, there aren't as many chuck wagons "out there" on the prairie as there once was, any more than there are as many Indians, buffalo, or cowboys, the still-existent large expanses of grazing land, with some difficult terrain, the rising cost of gas, and, even, long-standing tradition, still keeps the portable cowboy kitchen a viable part of the USA western landscape—even if it's more apt to be spotted these days being used to entertain greenhorns on dude ranches, and/or taking part in the chuck-wagon races which pretty much remain standard events at rodeos everywhere.

The following recipe comes to you, in a roundabout way, via a working chuck-wagon, from which I was first served these short ribs at the conclusion of a very tiring, dusty day of cattle wrangling on a ranch in the southwestern U.S.A. Luckily for me and for you, though, I was later served the same meal at the ranch house, and came away with today's modified recipe (just as delicious) that doesn't require us to dig holes in our yards, light fires in them, and, then, for several hours slowly pit-roast enough beef to feed a whole passel of hungry cowpokes.

### Ranch-House Short Ribs

6 lb short ribs (with bones)
Kosher salt
Pepper, freshly ground
Olive oil
1 large onion, roughly chopped
2 celery stalks, cut into approx ½-inch pieces
4 carrots, peeled, cut into approx ½-inch pieces
2 cloves garlic, chopped
1½ c tomato paste
2 to 3 c burgundy wine

½ c brown sugar
2 TBS Worcestershire sauce
1 TBS chili powder
2 sprigs fresh thyme and 2 of rosemary, tied together with kitchen string
2 c beef stock or water

Season each short rib generously with salt and pepper.

Coat a large pan with olive oil and heat on medium-high heat.

Brown on all sides, about 2 to 3 minutes per side. Don't overcrowd pan (cook in batches, if necessary).

As the short ribs are browning, puree all the vegetables and garlic in a food processor until it forms a coarse paste.

When all ribs are brown on all sides, remove them from the pan and put in a slow cooker (Crockpot®), turned on high. Set aside.

Drain the fat from pan in which the ribs were browned, leaving only enough to coat the bottom of pan.

Add the pureed vegetables to pan.

Generously season vegetables with salt and pepper.

Cook vegetables until very dark brown (about 5 to 7 minutes), scraping the bottom of the pan often.

Add the tomato paste to the pan and cook until the tomato paste is slightly brown (about 4 to 5 minutes), careful not to burn.

Whisk in wine to deglaze the pan.

Add brown sugar, Worcestershire sauce, and chili powder to pan, stirring to blend.

Cook, reducing mixture by half, watching carefully not to burn (lower the heat if necessary).

Place thyme and rosemary bundle in pan and immediately pour contents of pan over ribs in slow cooker.

Add 2 cups beef stock or water to slow cooker, until the meat is almost covered.

Cover and cook about 6 hours on high (or, according to slow cooker's directions).

Serve ribs in their accompanying sauce.

NOTE: As you might have guessed, I didn't supplement my original meal of this, out on the range, with any kind of fancy wine. I drank water, with an occasional swig of not-very-good whiskey from a fellow cow-hand's antique silver flask. At the ranch house, it was served up with all sorts of beer that was packed in amongst all sorts of ice, in one of those old-fashioned tin bathing tubs; the kind you picture Wyatt Earp having used. Since then, while I've enjoyed this with Pommard, Clos des Epeneaux, Comte Armand, Côte de Beaune, 1er cru, 2004, I'm always delighted when a certain friend of mine, as fond of this dish as I am, invites me over and supplements it with Hearty Burgundy, from the California USA Gallo winery; which continues to be one of my favorite inexpensive US wines.

# ADVANTAGING BOG AND PATCH

Cape Cod, known to the locals simply as "The Cape," is a "hook" of eastern Massachusetts State, northeastern USA landscape, which extends into the Atlantic Ocean.

A lot of people will recognize it as the location of the affluent summer resorts, Provincetown (P'town, for short, with its reputation for catering to vacationing gays), and Martha's Vineyard, the latter including the smaller Chappaquiddick Island made infamous by a certain 18 July 1969 car crash wherein U.S. Senator Edward M. ("Ted") Kennedy drove his automobile off Dike Bridge, fatally trapped his passenger, Mary Jo Kopechne, inside, and, then, fled the scene to provide scandal and world headlines.

Were I to mention any favorite recipes I happened to pick up while visiting there, I suspect, nine times out of ten, I'd have everyone thinking that I was talking about some tasty dish prepared from one of the area's renown denizens of the deep—striped bass, bluefish, sea bass, squid, giant bluefin tuna, and/or even the Cape's namesake "cod." And, in fact, I do have some favorites made from each and every one of those.

However, the favorite recipe of mine, brought along for your eating enjoyment, derives from the Cape Cod connection with two native North American foods—the pumpkin, and the cranberry—both of which are indigenous to this U.S. geological region that's only a stone's throw away from where, in 1620, the Pilgrims stepped ashore at fabled Plymouth Rock.

Before Cape Cod, I'd gathered pumpkins before, merely a case of strolling a farmer's field, where the orange globular fruit (and, yes, as a fleshy plant that has seeds and comes from a flower, it is a fruit), lie all around for picking up off the ground and dislodging from autumn-withered umbilical-cord vines. Harvesting cranberries, which takes place once a year from mid-September through early November, was a more unique experiences for me, in that, up until my close-up-and-personal encounter with them in Cape Cod, most of my berry picking had been done by hand, from other-than-cranberry dry-ground-grown bushes, not while wearing waders, up to my thighs in a flooded "bog", while water reels (egg-beaters) stirred up the water, dislodged the cranberries from their vines to have me using a plastic broom to help float them toward a suction hose and conveyor belt.

Having used the cranberries from my first official harvest, combined with some pumpkin acquired from a nearby patch, my Cape Cod host, mixed up a batch of cranberry-pumpkin "bread" from the recipe I still use, to this day, to whip up loaves of the same, for snacking, whenever I can.

## Berry-Good Pumpkin Bread

2 eggs, slightly beaten
2 c sugar
½ c vegetable oil
1 c pumpkin puree
2¼ c all-purpose flour
2 tsp pumpkin-pie spice
1 tsp soda
½ tsp salt
1 c fresh cranberries, roughly chopped
1 c powdered sugar (optional)

Preheat oven to 350°F.

Combine the eggs, sugar, and vegetable oil, mixing well.

Add pumpkin puree, mix, and set aside.

In a separate bowl, sift flour, pumpkin-pie spice, soda, and salt.

Add sifted ingredients to pumpkin mixture, and stir until dry ingredients are moist.

Fold in cranberries.

Spoon batter into 2 large loaf pans, or 4 small loaf pans, or a Bundt pan.

Bake for 1 hour.

TO MAKE A GLAZE, should you so desire: add enough water to a cup of powered sugar for a thin drizzle for the top of the bread.

NOTE: Sparkling wines usually go well with this, as does a crisp Sauvignon Blanc. Or, if you're up to experimenting, try a sweet dessert wine, like a Muscat.

## WHERE? AND EATING WHAT?

A lot of my recipes are indicative of the countries wherein I first discovered them. I'm sure there were no gasps of, "You don't say!" when it just so happened that my recipe for "Tortilla-Seraped Chipotle Black Bean Burritos" came via a trip to Mexico, and/or my recipe for "Goalie Ravioli" was the result of time I spent in Italy. In fact, I, more often than not, make a conscious effort to search out those recipes made of indigenous ingredients—something made of lemons in a country known for its lemons, or of oranges in a country known for its oranges, or of lamb in a country known for its lamb, or of beef in a country known for its beef—if just because chefs, the world round, are often best at utilizing whatever produce of which they have plenty and of which they often have conveniently near to hand.

The recipe highlighted in this chapter is an exception. I happened to be in Seoul, South Korea, at the time, on the tail end of a culinary adventure that had seen me sampling marinated galbi (pork ribs in Korean soy sauce), Kongguksa (noodles in cold soy milk), Sannakji (live octopus cut into small pieces and served while it was still squiggling on the plate). My charming hostess was convinced I'd likely overdosed on Korean cuisine, by the time I'd arrived in her kitchen, and that I had likely grown nostalgic for some home-made U.S.A. cooking. She'd gone out of her way and comfort zone to improvise a dish that she figured I'd welcome, by way of change...even though the panko she used in the dish she served was neither American nor Korean, but Japanese; and the T-bone steaks were from Korean native cattle, Hanwoo, initially raised as draft animals and not, before extensive crossbreeding, for supplying meat for anyone's dining-room table.

The result was downright delicious and remains something I usually serve up with the accompanying question, "Now, just where in the world do you think I was when I came across this?"

### "T" for Three

4 TBS butter
3 garlic cloves, minced
¾ c beef stock
½ c hardy red wine
½ c bleu cheese, coarsely crumbled
¼ c panko (Japanese breadcrumbs)
3 one-inch-thick T-bone steaks
Salt and pepper to taste

Melt 1 TBS butter in heavy, medium skillet over medium-high heat. Turn heat to low.

Add garlic and sauté for about 5 minutes.

Add stock and wine. Bring to a boil. Reduce sauce to ½ c (approx 10 minutes).

Set sauce aside.

Thoroughly blend bleu cheese and panko together in a small bowl. Cover. Chill. Set aside.

(NOTE: Sauce and the cheese/panko mixture can be made the day before.)

Sprinkle steaks with salt and pepper.

Melt 2 TBS butter in heavy large skillet over medium-high heat.

Cook steaks to nearly desired doneness, remembering they'll cook even more when put under the broiler.

Preheat broiler.

Transfer steaks to rimmed baking sheet.

Dividing the cheese mixture into three equal parts, press it on top of the steaks.

Broil the cheese-topped steaks until cheese browns (approx 2 minutes).

Transfer steaks to plates.

Pour sauce into the pan in which the steaks were last cooked and bring sauce to boil, scraping up browned bits.

Boil 2 minutes.

Whisk in remaining 1 TBS butter.

If desired, season sauce with additional salt and pepper to taste.

Spoon sauce over steaks and serve.

NOTE: My South Korean hostess had advantaged diplomatic connections to obtain and serve this with a California "Hook and Ladder Third Alarm Cabernet Sauvignon Reserve", which I found an excellent choice, I've since substituted all manner of Cabernet Sauvignons (Californian and otherwise) and found most of them to have provided good pairings.

# CIAO, COLUMBUS!

Let's all take a quick moment to give thanks to Christopher Columbus who not only discovered the Americas (although, yes, there is now some argument that there were those who did it before him), but who is certainly responsible for so many indigenous New World foods—think avocado, beans, bell pepper, blueberry, cacao, cashew, cassava root, chili pepper, corn, peanut, pecan, pineapple, pumpkin, potato, sunflower, tomato, vanilla, wild rice—becoming staples, too, of the Old World.

Today, let's specifically thank him for beginning the trip of the North American squash to Italy for its eventual evolution, once there, into what we now know today as zucchini. While, in the culinary world, zucchini is treated as a vegetable, inevitably ending up in savory dishes, or as accompaniments, it's botanically a fruit, having morphed from the swollen ovary of the plant's flower. It's one of those things that can be expected to be included among those items from just about any basket of produce delivered to one's doorstep, these days, by gracious friends and/or acquaintances who actually grow their own gardens.

"Zucchini à la Zimella" is what's on our menu.

Not that I can tell you all that much about the little Italian town of Zimella. In truth, I only realized I'd been there when I was reminded that I'd spent a festive evening at its DNA Disco Club, at the end of a road trip from and to Verona, with a group of dance-happy friends.

Zucchini à la Zimella was not actually eaten by me first-time in Zimella, but in Milan where it was served up by the son of a Zimella-born Italian Mama who had passed on her recipe.

So, as coincidence would have it, let's give thanks to Christopher-Adolfo, Italian son, not only for his having prepared it for me while he was still on his adrenaline high from, as a model, having walked the runways of two Milan fashion shows in one day (which had pooped me out from just watching), but who, then, graciously obliged by handing over (among other things) his Mama's treasured recipe.

### Zucchini à la Zimella

2 medium zucchini
Salt
1 lb ground beef
1 lb Italian sausage
1 medium onion, diced
1 garlic clove, minced
1 c cooked brown rice
1 TBS Italian seasoning
1 tsp salt

1 egg, beaten
2 (14-oz) cans petite-cut tomatoes
mozzarella or cheese of your choice (optional), grated

Preheat oven to 350°F.

Grease baking sheet-with-sides.

Cut zucchini in half, lengthwise. Scoop out seeds and some of the flesh, leaving ¾-inch of the flesh all around.

Sprinkle zucchini halves with salt and set aside.

Chop the seeds.

In a bowl, mix together all additional ingredients, including chopped seeds, but excluding optional cheese.

Divide the resulting mixture into the two hollowed zucchini half-shells.

Bake at preheated oven for about 45 minutes.

Optional: During the last 5 minutes of baking, top with grated mozzarella cheese, or a cheese of your choice.

NOTE: By way of a wine pairing, try a Cabernet Sauvignon, Barolo, or Shiraz. Possibly even a Pinot Noir.

# EATING THE VOLCANO

On 13 November 1985, after sixty-nine years of dormancy, the volcano known as *Nevado del Ruiz* erupted in the country of Colombia, South America, melting its mountaintop glaciers, and proceeding to bury several towns beneath the resulting onrushes of pyroclastic flows and lahars (volcanically induced mudslides), that came barreling down the mountainside.

The following chocolate mud-cake recipe comes to you via my South American host who served it up to me one evening over coffee at his home outside of Lérida, Colombia, not all that far (as the crow flies) from the resulting tragedy of *Nevado del Ruiz*; the dessert having resulted by way of culinary in memoriam.

A second point of interest is how Colombia ranks as the third South American country, after Brazil and Ecuador, by way of cacao bean production, but since its demand exceeds its locally produced supply, it ends up importing 30% of its yearly cocoa consumption. Therefore, any chocolate served up to you in Colombia has a one in three chance of not being indigenous to the country in which you're eating it.

That brings us to how this dessert ideally doesn't end up being made from South American cacao beans at all but from those originating in Africa's "Gold Coast" and packaged as the Xoçai Healthy Chocolate Nuggets® with which I'd gifted my host before he turned them over to his cook for incorporation in the resulting final recipe.

As a hearty advocate of Xoçai Healthy Chocolate®, which is cold-pressed, rather than heat-processed, thereby retaining far more of its vital nutrients than ordinary chocolate (candy), I'm always gifting my friends with the product as well as making conscious efforts to pass on whatever recipes can successfully be adapted for it.

[For more information on Xoçai chocolate, and for purchasing it, for cooking and/or eating purposes, go on-line to Richesinchocolate.com ].

**Nevado del Ruiz Barro Pastel**

10 Xoçai Healthy Chocolate Nuggets®
½ c butter
1 TBS red wine (Merlot a good choice)
1 tsp vanilla
1 c confectioner's sugar (plus some additional for "dusting")
2 eggs, plus 1 additional yolk
6 TBS flour
1 tsp cinnamon

Preheat oven 425°F.

Butter 4 six-oz custard soufflé cups.

Melt the Nuggets and the butter in a microwavable bowl on high until butter is melted (about 1 minute).

Whisk until chocolate is completely melted.

Stir in wine, vanilla, and 1 cup confectioner's sugar until blended.

Add the eggs, plus one additional yolk.

Blend in the flour and cinnamon.

Divide mixture evenly between the buttered cups.

Bake for 13 to 15 minutes, until edges are firm but center is still soft.

Let stand for 1 minute.

Loosen edges with a knife.

Invert on to a dessert plate.

Sprinkle with confectioner's sugar.

Serve immediately.

Serves 4.

NOTE: This is a great dessert to serve with coffee. That

said...I recently experimented eating it with a red wine (7 Deadly Sins Zinfandel), a white wine (St. Chapelle Soft White), and Champagne (Veuve Clicquot), all three of which paired quite nicely with it.

# PICNICKING AT CHÂTEAU DE VERSAILLES

Admittedly, I have three fetishes. Waterfalls; why I never go to Argentina or Brazil without visiting Iguaçu. Greco-Roman statuary; why I never go to Italy without visiting the Musei Vaticani. Mirrors (although not as much as I used to when the reflections I received back were of a far-younger me); why I never go to France without visiting the wondrous Grande Galerie or Galerie des Glaces, the central gallery of the Château of Versailles, just outside Paris, and one of the most famous "spaces" in the world, and site of an orgy scene in my m/m novel, *I DEBAUCHEE*.

Of course, there are other reasons why I wouldn't miss Versailles. The Château, built when Versailles was a mere country village, now having become a suburb of Paris, located twenty kilometers southwest of the French capital, became the center of French political power from 1682, when Louis XIV moved there. It remained as such until Louis XVI and his family, including his infamous queen, Marie Antoinette, were forced to return to Paris in October 1789. This was after the commencement of the French

Revolution with its advocates ballyhooing, and acting out, their off-with-their-heads mentality. The Château and grounds remain prime examples of conspicuous consumption, including the Orangerie, built by Jules Hardouin-Mansart, still housing more than a thousand orange trees, each in its own huge planter, that only end up outdoors from May to October, in the Château's Parterre Bas, during the summertime when French weather won't kill them.

The first oranges were likely introduced to Europe in the fifteenth century, and were such an expensive food item that medieval rulebooks firmly stated just how many orange "slices" could be designated to each visiting dignitary.

And believe me when I tell you that there are few as spectacular locales in which to picnic than is offered by the Château grounds. Dining alfresco there, on an immaculate tablecloth spread upon manicured verdant lawn, during the toasty warmth of a French summer, remains one of my very favorite pastimes, especially when the picnic baskets—yes, inevitably more than one when dining with my favorite French hostess—are filled with such wondrously marvelous French gourmet items as crusty fresh bread topped by Fig and Olive Tapenade, Shrimp Salad, Country Cassoulet, Duck à l'Orange, Fricassee of Rabbit, Brie with White Truffles, all served up on Limoges fine porcelain, along with chilled Dom Perignon Champagne in Baccarat crystal flutes.

Did I mention dessert? A favorite of mine is an

orange cake which I refuse to call by any other name, these days, than "Let Them Eat Cake" Cake, since that name seems so apropos, considering I first ate this orange-flavored dessert on the grounds of Versailles, not long after visiting the Orangerie; the Château's one-time resident, Queen Marie Antoinette, supposedly having muttered (although since found NOT to have been the case) "Let them eat cake!" when told the French people were starving and unable to eat bread.

### "Let Them Eat Cake" Cake

(By the way, this cake is better the longer it sits. I always make it two days before I plan to serve it)

2¼ c sifted cake flour
1½ c sugar
2 tsps baking powder
¼ tsp soda
1 tsp salt
½ c shortening
Zest of one orange (approx. 1 tsp)
Juice from one orange (about ¼ c), plus water or milk to equal 1 c of liquid (the more orange juice the better)
2 eggs

Preheat oven to 350°F.

Prepare two 8-inch round cake pans.

Sift together in a bowl the flour, sugar, baking powder, soda, and salt.

Add shortening, orange zest, and ⅔ cup orange juice with water and/or milk.

Mix slowly, medium speed (about 2 minutes), scraping bowl often.

Add remaining liquid and eggs.

Continue beating 2 minutes more.

Bake 30 minutes, or until tester comes out clean.

Frosting:

2½ TBS cake flour
½ c milk
½ c butter
½ c sugar
¼ tsp salt
½ tsp vanilla
½ c walnuts, finely chopped
1 c powdered sugar, sifted

Into flour, gradually whisk in milk.

Cook to a very thick paste over low to medium low heat (about 10 minutes).

Set aside to cool to lukewarm.

Meanwhile, cream butter with sugar and salt.

Add previously prepared lukewarm paste.

Beat until fluffy.

Fold in vanilla and nuts.

Use about ⅓ of this mixture for filling between the layers.

To the remainder, blend in the powdered sugar.

Frost the two-tiered cake layers.

NOTE: I can't remember ever serving this cake with anything other than very good vintage French Champagne. However, I readily admit to that being an affectation to which no one, not nostalgic about picnicking on Versailles Château grounds with this dessert and Dom Perignon as part of that menu, need ever entertain. I suspect any Champagne or Sparkling-Wine equivalent would suffice, quite nicely, for anyone...but, maybe, me.

# ABOUT THE AUTHORS

**WILLIAM MALTESE** is the author...(with Bonnie Clark) of *BACK OF THE BOAT GOURMET COOKING* and *EVEN GOURMANDS HAVE TO DIET*...; (with Cecile Charles) *DINNER WITH CECILE AND WILLIAM*...; (with A. B. Gayle) *WILLIAM MALTESE'S WINE TASTER'S DIARY: IN SEARCH OF THE PERFECT G ON AUSTRALIA'S MORNINGTON PENINSULA*...; (with Adrienne Z. Milligan), *THE GLUTEN-FREE WAY: MY WAY*...; (with Christina-Marie Wright) *GET-REAL VEGAN DESSERTS*...; and his *WILLIAM MALTESE'S WINE TASTER'S DIARY: SPOKANE AND PULLMAN, WASHINGTON*—all for "The Traveling Gourmand" series of Borgo Press. He was born in the Pacific Northwest region of the U.S.A., has a B.A. in Marketing/Advertising, and spent an honorable tour of duty in the U.S. Army where he achieved the rank of E-5. He started his career writing for men's pulp magazines, and has since had published more than 200 books, fiction and nonfiction, in every genre, while being honored with a listing in the prestigious *Who's Who in America*. For more information on William, pick up a copy of:

*DRAQUALIAN SILK: A COLLECTOR'S AND BIBLIOGRAPHICAL GUIDE TO THE BOOKS OF WILLIAM MALTESE 1969-2010*

...available in book stores everywhere.

And check out his websites:

williammaltese.com
facebook.com/williammaltese
theglutenfreewaymyway.com/
facebook.com/backoftheboatgourmetcooking
facebook.com/winetastersdiary
facebook.com/DinnerWithCecileAndWilliamACookbook?fref=ts
facebook.com/evengourmandshavetodiet
facebook.com/flickerwarriors
facebook.com/draqual
myspace.com/williammaltese
myspace.com/draqual
myspace.com/flickerwarriors
William's Xocai® chocolate site:
mxi.myvoffice.com/williammaltese/

**BONNIE** and her husband Bruce were born, raised, met, and married in the Spokane, Washington, U.S.A. area, and have since raised their family there. Bonnie's interest in cooking began at a very early age when her Mother went to work, and Bonnie started planning and preparing dinners for the family. Her passion for cooking and entertaining grew, bolstered by her close connection and participation in her mother-in-law's professional catering business. Finally, enough family and friends told her she "should write a cookbook" that she decided, maybe, it was time she did. As it happens, her cousin, help- and cook-book author, William Maltese, fellow gourmand, wine connoisseur, and avid boater, was looking to do the same thing, and BACK OF THE BOAT GOURMET COOKING was born, followed by EVEN GOURMANDS NEED TO DIET. The latter contains some common-sense observations on dieting from two people daily subjected to good food, good wine, and the necessity to count calories.

Check out her other websites:

facebook.com/bclarkchocolate
facebook.com/backoftheboatgourmetcooking
facebook.com/evengourmandshavetodiet

Bonnie's Xocai® chocolate-for-sale site:

richesinchocolate.com

www.ingramcontent.com/pod-product-compliance
Lightning Source LLC
LaVergne TN
LVHW041628070426
835507LV00008B/502